YOUR PERSONAL
ASTROLOGY
GUIDE

GEMINI
2012

YOUR PERSONAL
ASTROLOGY
GUIDE

GEMINI
2012

RICK LEVINE **& JEFF** JAWER

STERLING ETHOS
New York

STERLING ETHOS
New York

**An Imprint of Sterling Publishing
387 Park Avenue South
New York, NY 10016**

STERLING ETHOS and the distinctive Sterling logo are registered trademarks of Sterling Publishing Co., Inc.

© 2011 Sterling Publishing Co., Inc.
Text © 2011 by Rick Levine and Jeff Jawer

All rights reserved. No part of this publication may be reproduced, stored in a retrieval system, or transmitted, in any form or by any means, electronic, mechanical, photocopying, recording, or otherwise, without prior written permission from the publisher.

ISBN 978-1-4027-7946-6 (print format)
ISBN 978-1-4027-8916-8 (ebook)

Distributed in Canada by Sterling Publishing
^{c}/o Canadian Manda Group, 165 Dufferin Street
Toronto, Ontario, Canada M6K 3H6
Distributed in the United Kingdom by GMC Distribution Services
Castle Place, 166 High Street, Lewes, East Sussex, England BN7 1XU
Distributed in Australia by Capricorn Link (Australia) Pty. Ltd.
P.O. Box 704, Windsor, NSW 2756, Australia

For information about custom editions, special sales, and premium and corporate purchases, please contact Sterling Special Sales at 800-805-5489 or specialsales@sterlingpublishing.com.

Printed in Canada

2 4 6 8 10 9 7 5 3 1

www.sterlingpublishing.com

TABLE OF CONTENTS

Introduction	7
Moon Charts	11
CHAPTER I: ASTROLOGY, YOU & THE WORLD	15
CHAPTER 2: GEMINI AUGUST–DECEMBER 2011 OVERVIEW	35
CHAPTER 3: 2012 HOROSCOPE	46

APPENDIXES

2012 Month-at-a-Glance Astrocalendar	131
Famous Geminis	143
Gemini in Love	145
About the Authors	158
Acknowledgments	159

Author's Note:

Your Personal Astrology Guide uses the Tropical zodiac based on the seasons, not the constellations. This method of determining signs has been and continues to be the practice of Western astrologers for over 2,000 years. Aries, the beginning of the Tropical zodiac, starts on the first day of spring every year. Contrary to what you may have heard, no one's sign has changed, regardless of when you were born and the addition of a thirteenth sign is not relevant to Western astrology.

Measuring and recording the apparent movement of the Sun, the Moon, and the planets against the backdrop of the heavens is a complex task because nothing is stationary. Even the location of the constellations with respect to the seasons gradually changes from year to year. Since astrologers are concerned with human behavior here on Earth, they created a twelve-fold zodiac that is anchored to four seasons as their primary frame of reference. Obviously, astrologers fully understand that there are eighty-eight official constellations and that the moving planets travel through many of them (including Ophiuchus and Orion), but these are not—and never have been—part of the Tropical zodiac created by astrologers.

INTRODUCTION

THE PURPOSE OF THIS BOOK

The more you learn about yourself, the better able you are to wisely use the energies in your life. For more than 3,000 years, astrology has been the sharpest tool in the box for describing the human condition. Used by virtually every culture on the planet, astrology continues to serve as a link between individual lives and planetary cycles. We gain valuable insights into personal issues with a birth chart, and can plot the patterns of the year ahead in meaningful ways for individuals as well as groups. You share your sun sign with eight percent of humanity. Clearly, you're not all going to have the same day, even if the basic astrological cycles are the same. Your individual circumstances, the specific factors of your entire birth chart, and your own free will help you write your unique story.

The purpose of this book is to describe the energies of the Sun, Moon, and planets for the year ahead and help you create your future, rather than being a victim of it. We aim to facilitate your journey by showing you the turns ahead in the road of life and hopefully the best ways to navigate them.

INTRODUCTION

YOU ARE THE STAR OF YOUR LIFE

It is not our goal to simply predict events. Rather, we are reporting the planetary energies—the cosmic weather in which you are living—so that you understand these conditions and know how to use them most effectively.

The power, though, isn't in the stars, but in your mind, your heart, and the choices that you make every day. Regardless of how strongly you are buffeted by the winds of change or bored by stagnation, you have many ways to view any situation. Learning about the energies of the Sun, Moon, and planets will both sharpen and widen your perspective, thereby giving you additional choices.

The language of astrology is a gift of awareness, not a rigid set of rules. It works best when blended with common sense, intuition, and self-trust. This is your life, and no one knows how to live it as well as you. Take what you need from this book and leave the rest. Although the planets set the stage for the year ahead, you're the writer, director, and star of

INTRODUCTION ♊

your life and you can play the part in whatever way you choose. *Your Personal Astrology Guide* uses information about your sun sign to give you a better understanding of how the planetary waves will wash upon your shore. We each navigate our lives through time, and each moment has unique qualities. Astrology gives us the ability to describe the constantly changing timescape. For example, if you know the trajectory and the speed of an approaching storm, you can choose to delay a leisurely afternoon sail on the bay, thus avoiding an unpleasant situation.

By reading this book, you can improve your ability to align with the cosmic weather, the larger patterns that affect you day to day. You can become more effective by aligning with the cosmos and cocreating the year ahead with a better understanding of the energies around you.

Astrology doesn't provide quick fixes to life's complex issues. It doesn't offer neatly packed black-and-white answers in a world filled with an infinite variety of shapes and colors. It can, however, give you a much clearer picture of the invisible forces influencing your life.

INTRODUCTION

ENERGY & EVENTS

Two sailboats can face the same gale yet travel in opposite directions as a result of how the sails are positioned. Similarly, how you respond to the energy of a particular set of circumstances may be more responsible for your fate than the given situation itself. We delineate the energetic winds for your year ahead, but your attitude shapes the unfolding events, and your responses alter your destiny.

This book emphasizes the positive, not because all is good, but because astrology shows us ways to transform even the power of a storm into beneficial results. Empowerment comes from learning to see the invisible energy patterns that impact the visible landscape as you fill in the details of your story every day on this spinning planet, orbited by the Moon, lit by the Sun, and colored by the nuances of the planets.

You are a unique point in an infinite galaxy of unlimited possibilities, and the choices that you make have consequences. So use this book in a most magical way to consciously improve your life.

MOON CHARTS

MOON CHARTS

2012 NEW MOONS

Each New Moon marks the beginning of a cycle. In general, this is the best time to plant seeds for future growth. Use the days preceding the New Moon to finish old business prior to starting what comes next. The focused mind can be quite sharp during this phase. Harness the potential of the New Moon by stating your intentions—out loud or in writing—for the weeks ahead. Hold these goals in your mind and help them grow to fruition through conscious actions as the Moon gains light during the following two weeks. In the chart below, the dates and times refer to when the Moon and Sun align in each zodiac sign (see p. 16), initiating a new lunar cycle.

DATE	TIME	SIGN
January 23	2:39 am EST	Aquarius
February 21	5:34 pm EST	Pisces
March 22	10:37 am EDT	Aries
April 21	3:18 am EDT	Taurus
May 20	7:47 pm EDT	Gemini (ECLIPSE)
June 19	11:02 am EDT	Gemini
July 19	12:24 am EDT	Cancer
August 17	11:54 am EDT	Leo
September 15	10:10 pm EDT	Virgo
October 15	8:02 am EDT	Libra
November 13	5:07 pm EST	Scorpio (ECLIPSE)
December 13	3:41 am EST	Sagittarius

MOON CHARTS   ♊

2012 FULL MOONS

The Full Moon reflects the light of the Sun as subjective feelings reflect the objective events of the day. Dreams seem bigger; moods feel stronger. Emotional waters run with deeper currents. This is the phase of culmination, a turning point in the energetic cycle. Now it's time to listen to the inner voices. Rather than starting new projects, the two weeks after the Full Moon are when we complete what we can and slow our outward expressions in anticipation of the next New Moon. In this chart, the dates and times refer to when the moon is opposite the sun in each zodiac sign, marking the emotional peak of each lunar cycle.

DATE	TIME	SIGN
January 9	2:30 am EST	Cancer
February 7	4:53 pm EST	Leo
March 8	4:39 am EST	Virgo
April 6	3:18 pm EDT	Libra
May 5	11:35 pm EDT	Scorpio
June 4	7:11 am EDT	Sagittarius (ECLIPSE)
July 3	2:51 pm EDT	Capricorn
August 1	11:27 pm EDT	Aquarius
August 31	9:58 am EDT	Pisces
September 29	11:18 pm EDT	Aries
October 29	3:49 pm EDT	Taurus
November 28	9:45 am EST	Gemini (ECLIPSE)
December 28	5:21 am EST	Cancer

ASTROLOGY, YOU & THE WORLD

WELCOME TO YOUR SUN SIGN

The Sun, Moon, and Earth and all the planets lie within a plane called the **ecliptic** and move through a narrow band of stars made up by 12 constellations called the **zodiac**. The Earth revolves around the Sun once a year, but from our point of view, it appears that the Sun moves through each sign of the zodiac for one month. There are 12 months and astrologically there are 12 signs. The astrological months, however, do not match our calendar, and start between the 19th and 23rd of each month. Everyone is born to an astrological month, like being born in a room with a particular perspective of the world. Knowing your sun sign provides useful information about your personality and your future, but for a more detailed astrological analysis, a full birth chart calculation based on your precise date, time, and place of birth is necessary. Get your complete birth chart online at:

http://www.tarot.com/astrology/astroprofile

ASTROLOGY, YOU & THE WORLD ♊

This book is about your zodiac sign. Your Sun is in the air sign of curious Gemini, the Twins. For you, life presents itself as a spectrum of possibilities, and you tune in to and out of experiences as if you were listening to a radio. Duality is your theme; there is always an alternate station. At your worst, you might be scattered, but your greatest strengths are your active mind, your cleverness with words, and the ability to think on your feet.

THE PLANETS

We refer to the Sun and Moon as planets. Don't worry; we do know about modern astronomy. Although the Sun is really a star and the Moon is a satellite, they are called planets for astrological purposes. The astrological planets are the Sun, the Moon, Mercury, Venus, Mars, Jupiter, Saturn, Chiron, Uranus, Neptune, and Pluto.

Your sun sign is the most obvious astrological placement, for the Sun returns to the same sign every year. But at the same time, the Moon is orbiting the Earth, changing signs every two and a third days. Mercury, Venus, and Mars each move through a sign in a few weeks to a few months.

GEMINI 2012

Jupiter spends a whole year in a sign—and Pluto visits a sign for up to 30 years! The ever-changing positions of the planets alter the energetic terrain through which we travel. The planets are symbols; each has a particular range of meanings. For example, Venus is the goddess of love, but it really symbolizes beauty in a spectrum of experiences. Venus can represent romantic love, sensuality, the arts, or good food. It activates anything that we value, including personal possessions and even money. To our ancestors, the planets actually animated life on Earth. In this way of thinking, every beautiful flower contains the essence of Venus.

Each sign has a natural affinity to an individual planet, and as this planet moves through the sky, it sends messages of particular interest to people born under that sign. Your key or ruling planet is Mercury, the Messenger of the Heavens. Quicksilver Mercury is the fastest of the true planets, symbolic of the speed and changeability of thought. Its function is to send and receive data through all forms of intelligible communication. Its movement shows the qualities of your thinking process and speech. Planets can be described by many different words, for the mythology of each is a rich tapestry. In this book we use a variety of words when talking about each planet in order to convey the most applicable meaning. The table below describes a few keywords for each planet, including the Sun and Moon.

PLANET	SYMBOL	KEYWORDS
Sun	☉	Consciousness, Will, Vitality
Moon	☽	Subconscious, Emotions, Habits
Mercury	☿	Communication, Thoughts, Transportation
Venus	♀	Desire, Love, Money, Values
Mars	♂	Action, Physical Energy, Drive
Jupiter	♃	Expansion, Growth, Optimism
Saturn	♄	Contraction, Maturity, Responsibility
Chiron	⚷	Healing, Pain, Subversion
Uranus	♅	Awakening, Unpredictable, Inventive
Neptune	♆	Imagination, Spirituality, Confusion
Pluto	♇	Passion, Intensity, Regeneration

HOUSES

Just as planets move through the signs of the zodiac, they also move through the houses in an individual chart. The 12 houses correspond to the 12 signs, but are individualized, based upon your

GEMINI 2012

sign. In this book we use Solar Houses, which place your sun sign in your 1st House. Therefore, when a planet enters a new sign it also enters a new house. If you know your exact time of birth, the rising sign determines the 1st House. You can learn your rising sign by entering your birth date at:

http://www.tarot.com/astrology/astroprofile

HOUSE	SIGN	KEYWORDS
1st House	Aries	Self, Appearance, Personality
2nd House	Taurus	Possessions, Values, Self-Worth
3rd House	Gemini	Communication, Siblings, Short Trips
4th House	Cancer	Home, Family, Roots
5th House	Leo	Love, Romance, Children, Play
6th House	Virgo	Work, Health, Daily Routines
7th House	Libra	Marriage, Relationships, Business Partners
8th House	Scorpio	Intimacy, Transformation, Shared Resources
9th House	Sagittarius	Travel, Higher Education, Philosophy
10th House	Capricorn	Career, Community, Ambition
11th House	Aquarius	Groups and Friends, Associations, Social Ideals
12th House	Pisces	Imagination, Spirituality, Secret Activities

ASTROLOGY, YOU & THE WORLD

ASPECTS

As the planets move through the sky in their various cycles, they form ever-changing angles with one another. Certain angles create significant geometric shapes. So, when two planets are 90 degrees apart, they conform to a square; 60 degrees of separation conforms to a sextile, or six-pointed star. Planets create **aspects** when they're at these special angles. Aspects explain how the individual symbolism of pairs of planets combine into an energetic pattern.

ASPECT	DEGREES	KEYWORD
Conjunction	0	Compression, Blending, Focus
Opposition	180	Tension, Awareness, Balance
Trine	120	Harmony, Free-Flowing, Ease
Square	90	Resistance, Stress, Dynamic Conflict
Quintile	72	Creativity, Metaphysical, Magic
Sextile	60	Support, Intelligent, Activating
Quincunx	150	Irritation, Annoyance, Adjustment

2012 GENERAL FORECAST

Astrology works for individuals, groups, and humanity as a whole. You will have your own story in 2012, but it will unfold along with seven billion other tales of human experience. We are each unique, yet our lives touch one another; our destinies are woven together by weather and war, by the economy, science, music, politics, religion, and all the other threads of life on planet Earth.

This astrological look at the major trends and planetary patterns for 2012 provides a framework for comprehending the potentials and challenges we face together, so that we can move forward with tolerance and respect as a community as we also fulfill our potential as individuals.

The astrological events used for this forecast are the transits of major planets Jupiter and Saturn, the retrograde cycles of Mercury, and the eclipses of the Sun and the Moon.

ASTROLOGY, YOU & THE WORLD

A NOTE ABOUT DATES IN THIS BOOK

All events are based upon the Eastern Time Zone of the United States. Because of local time differences, an event occurring just a few minutes after midnight in the East will actually happen the prior day in the rest of the country. Although the key dates are the exact dates of any particular alignment, some of you are so ready for certain things to happen that you can react to a transit a day or two before it is exact. And sometimes you can be so entrenched in habits or unwilling to change that you may not notice the effects right away. Allow extra time around each key date to feel the impact of any event.

JUPITER IN TAURUS:
SUSTAINABLE GROWTH
June 4, 2011–June 11, 2012

New visions sparked by Jupiter in fiery Aries are now in the process of being tested by reality. Bright ideas come down to earth in sensible Taurus, where we can gain material benefits from recent discoveries. A practical approach to progress enables us to make incremental improvements that will endure. Viable sources of cheaper and cleaner energy reflect the gifts of generous Jupiter in this resource-rich sign.

However, we may be more stubborn and resistant to unfamiliar ideas, and a selfish desire for wealth can close minds to inspiring concepts if they take time to turn a profit. Philosophical Jupiter in fixed Taurus narrows our intellectual comfort zone, so we may not be inclined to ask provocative questions that challenge our core beliefs.

JUPITER IN GEMINI:
INFORMATION OVERLOAD
June 11, 2012–June 25, 2013

Astrological tradition considers multifaceted Gemini an awkward place for truth-seeking Jupiter. We can be inundated with so much information that it's nearly impossible to see the forest for the trees. Jupiter's long-range vision may be obscured by a million-and-one ideas that scatter attention, diffusing the focus we need to achieve long-term goals. However, this is a mind-opening transit that stirs curiosity about a wide variety of subjects. Still, a tendency to skim the surface makes it difficult to concentrate and gain in-depth knowledge in any one area. Expansive Jupiter in communicative Gemini can also be quite verbose—the volume of information is valued more than its substance. Nevertheless, we are able to assimilate large amounts of data and make interesting connections between previously unrelated points.

SATURN IN LIBRA:
JUSTICE FOR ALL
October 29, 2009–April 7, 2010
July 21, 2010–October 5, 2012

Stern Saturn's shift into peace-seeking Libra marked a new chapter in our relationships, but we still have some tough challenges to face before we can fully achieve the harmony it symbolizes. When Saturn in Libra functions at its highest potential, cooperation and civility allow diplomacy to flourish as reason replaces force. The need to weigh both sides of any argument can slow personal and public dialogue, yet it's worth the price to build bridges over seemingly impassable chasms. Saturn is "exalted" in Libra according to astrological tradition, suggesting a highly positive link between the planet's principle of integrity and Libra's sense of fair play. The negative side of Saturn, though, is its potential for rigidity, which can manifest now as a stubborn unwillingness to listen.

Karmic Saturn is judgmental and known to deliver exactly what we deserve. When it's in Libra the Scales, justice becomes one way of restoring balance. Accordingly, legal systems around the world may take steps to correct social inequities and governmental and corporate abuses of power.

SATURN IN SCORPIO:
LOOKING INTO THE SHADOWS
October 5, 2012–December 23, 2014
June 14, 2015–September 16, 2015

Responsible Saturn in formidable Scorpio is a test of resolve. We are challenged to look into the dark corners of our psyches where fears about love, money, and mortality hide. It's tempting to turn away from these complicated subjects, yet the price of doing so is high because we are then controlled by unconscious impulses. Power struggles and relationship disappointments are common when we fail to face emotional issues, no matter how intense they may seem. However, for those who are willing to show up and do the work, Saturn also offers clarity and authority, enabling us to address these complicated matters.

ASTROLOGY, YOU & THE WORLD

Discovering what we truly desire (and detest) is a powerful step toward creating healthier relationships. We may not get all our needs met, yet acknowledging them makes it possible to have an honest discussion and to negotiate in good faith.

MERCURY RETROGRADES
**March 12 in Aries, Direct April 4 in Pisces /
July 14–August 8 in Leo / November 6 in Sagittarius,
Direct November 26 in Scorpio**

All true planets appear to move backward from time to time, because we view them from the moving platform of Earth. The most noticeable and regular retrograde periods are those of Mercury, the communication planet. Occurring three or four times a year for roughly three weeks at a time, these are periods when difficulties with details, travel, communication, and technical matters are more common than usual.

Mercury's retrograde is often perceived as negative, but you can make this cycle work for you. Because personal and commercial interactions are emphasized, you can actually accomplish more than usual, especially if you stay focused on what you need to complete instead of initiating new projects. Still, you may feel as if you're treading water—or worse, being carried backward in an undertow of unfinished business. Worry less about making progress than about the quality of your work. Pay extra attention to all your communication exchanges. Avoiding misunderstandings and omissions is the ideal way to minimize complications. Retrograde Mercury is best used to tie up loose ends as you review, redo, reconsider, and, in general, revisit the past.

ECLIPSES
Solar: May 20 and November 13
Lunar: June 4 and November 28

Solar and Lunar Eclipses are special New and Full Moons that indicate significant changes for individuals and groups. They are powerful markers of events, with influences that can appear up to three months in advance and last up to six months afterward.

May 20, Solar Eclipse in Gemini: Lost in Space
This annular Solar Eclipse in Gemini is stressfully squared by nebulous Neptune, suggesting

confusion, scandals, and floods. Its trajectory stretches from the coast of China to the western United States, but its central path through Tokyo makes Japan the likeliest locale for a major event. Individually, it's a reminder that too much information can be just as disorienting as a lack of data. Neptune encourages idealism and spiritual pursuits, but we must exercise intelligent discrimination to avoid falling prey to a fantasy.

June 4, Lunar Eclipse in Sagittarius: Check the Facts

Relationships could be rocky with the eclipsed Moon opposing loving Venus and tensely squared by aggressive Mars. We can feel forced to make a decision before we're ready, yet the cavalier Sagittarius Moon encourages us to jump ahead before thinking about the consequences of our actions. Vital information may be missing, or communications could be so vague that coming to a rational conclusion is difficult. Back up, think things through carefully, ask more questions, and review recent conversations before making any serious commitments.

GEMINI 2012

November 13, Solar Eclipse in Scorpio:
Resistance Is Futile
This total eclipse of the Sun in resolute Scorpio is excellent for letting go of unhealthy habits. Deeply rooted obsessions can reach a critical point where it becomes evident that it's time to relinquish control. Financial and emotional pressures create a need to reassess priorities. This New Moon Eclipse is in an anxious semisquare to ruthless Pluto, increasing the stakes and decreasing our willingness to compromise. Stubbornly resisting change becomes detrimental and even destructive, reminding us to step back and measure the costs of our behavior with a much-needed dose of detachment.

November 28, Lunar Eclipse in Gemini: Baby Steps
Optimistic Jupiter's conjunction to the eclipsed Full Moon represents high hopes, yet a lack of resources might push them out of reach. Tight-fisted conjunctions of Venus and Saturn and Mars and Pluto demand fiscal restraint and careful time management. Meanwhile, maverick Chiron squares the restless Gemini Moon, provoking risky behavior in order to avoid a painful issue.

ASTROLOGY, YOU & THE WORLD

It's wise to avoid making big promises that might be difficult to deliver. We can either aim lower in our aspirations for the time being or prepare to work harder and longer to get where we want to go.

THE BOTTOM LINE:
BE THE CHANGE

The mainstream media have been sending fearful apocalyptic messages that 2012 is a year of monumental change because of the shift in the Mayan calendar on December 21. End-of-the-world predictions are nothing new and this one, like the others, is premature. In fact, there are several Mayan calendars ranging from one of 260 days to the Long Count Calendar of 5,126 years that turns over in December. It does not mark the end of time; it simply indicates the end of one cycle and the beginning of the next. While there are significant astrological patterns this year, the Mayan calendar doesn't correspond with them. Nevertheless, a general perception of dramatic change could contribute to making it a reality.

A major astrological pattern starts this year that won't finish until January 2015, indicating that we are in a period of significant transformation. Uranus, the planet of surprises and breakthroughs, forms seven disruptive squares with potent Pluto during a three-year period. They occur on June 24 and September 19, 2012, May 20 and November 1, 2013, April 21 and December 15, 2014, and March 16, 2015. This long-lasting connection between revolutionary Uranus and volcanic Pluto will foment change on a grand scale. This pair of change agents formed conjunctions in 1965 and 1966 that gave rise to the hopeful social movements around the globe that characterized this most memorable decade. The Uranus-Pluto squares that start this year are, in essence, the next step in the process that began nearly fifty years ago. Issues that arose then will spring back into collective awareness with a renewed sense of urgency that will again wake the masses and inspire radical action.

Uranus in innovative Aries is pushing against entrenched power represented by Pluto in Capricorn. But this is not simply a response to external authorities; it signals a significant shift in the sense of who we are. The mix of technology and medicine with rapid advances in genetic research make it possible to alter the human body and redirect our evolutionary path. The 1960s gave birth to liberation movements based on race, gender, and sexual preference that have gone a long way toward ending the old models of family and community. It was, like all revolutionary periods, marked by creativity and chaos, as well as freedom and fear. As we launch ourselves into a future of our own making, resistance is to be expected. Traditional institutions will condemn experimentation, and our own psyches will recoil against the forward thrust of history. Yet major changes are coming whether we accept them or not. Clearly, the powerful tides of time cannot be stopped. The wisest path is to participate with a spirit of innovation and the flexibility to adapt to unexpected events, as we lead humanity to the next stage of adventure and discovery.

    Remember that all of these astrological events are part of the general cosmic weather of the year, but will affect us each differently based upon our individual astrological signs.

GEMINI
AUGUST–DECEMBER
2011 OVERVIEW

GEMINI AUGUST 2011 OVERVIEW

PRACTICE MAKES PERFECT

The bold Leo Sun burns through your 3rd House of Communication until **August 23**, offering a brightly lit stage for expressing your ideas. You have plentiful opportunities to speak up, but you'd better rehearse your lines carefully to make the most of them. That's because Mercury will be retrograde **August 2–26**, a period when verbal mishaps occur more frequently. Think through any significant discussion—public or private—in advance to make sure that you're on point. Action-planet Mars enters hypersensitive Cancer on **August 3**, undercutting objectivity with feelings. This produces a more delicate environment in which mistakes won't be quickly forgotten or forgiven.

Charm can take you a long way on **August 13**, when the Full Moon in brilliant Aquarius opposes gracious Venus. Normally, this lunation in your opinionated 9th House is a time of mental breakthroughs and intellectual feats of strength. Right now, however, the focus is also on your heart; don't let big ideas get in the way of the small things that show others how much you care. Dutiful Saturn's squishy sesquisquare with illusory Neptune on **August 24**—the last in a series that began on **October 27, 2010**—confronts you with a choice between the real and the ideal. Still, it doesn't mean that you must discard your dreams or surrender your sense of responsibility. This aspect is a magical lesson in learning how to integrate the worlds of mind and matter. Mercury's direct turn on **August 26** and the competent Virgo New Moon on **August 28** reveal your readiness to develop these new skills.

AUGUST 2011

MONDAY 1

TUESDAY 2 ★ Pay attention to the tone of your words

WEDNESDAY 3 ★

THURSDAY 4 ★

FRIDAY 5

SATURDAY 6

SUNDAY 7

MONDAY 8 ★ Use this time creatively instead of forcing clarity

TUESDAY 9

WEDNESDAY 10

THURSDAY 11

FRIDAY 12

SATURDAY 13 ★ ○ **SUPER NOVA DAYS** Try saying no before going too far

SUNDAY 14 ★

MONDAY 15 ★

TUESDAY 16 ★

WEDNESDAY 17 ★

THURSDAY 18

FRIDAY 19

SATURDAY 20

SUNDAY 21 ★ Attend to your own needs before those of others

MONDAY 22 ★

TUESDAY 23 ★

WEDNESDAY 24 ★ Financial frustration leads to being fiscally resourceful

THURSDAY 25 ★

FRIDAY 26 ★

SATURDAY 27 ★

SUNDAY 28 ●

MONDAY 29

TUESDAY 30

WEDNESDAY 31

★ designates key date

GEMINI SEPTEMBER 2011 OVERVIEW

DUTIES AND DELIGHTS

A delicate dance between work and play demands your attention this month. The Sun in efficient Virgo requires you to do some personal cleanup and reorganization while it occupies your 4th House of Roots until **September 23**. Mercury's move into Virgo on **September 9** focuses your energy on what you need to fix at home and within your family. You're likely to be more self-critical now—but think of it as an opportunity to recognize unhealthy habits clearly enough that you can actually begin changing them. This can be a slow process because you're dealing with deeply rooted patterns that are just beginning to emerge into consciousness. The Full Moon on **September 12** in vulnerable Pisces and your 10th House of Career exposes your insecurities over work. Finding inspiration on the job or in other forms of public service can help to wash away your worries.

The playful side of the equation is emphasized when delightful Venus enters your 5th House of Fun and Games on **September 14**. Mars's shift into affectionate Leo on **September 18** and the Sun's move into amicable Libra and your 5th House on **September 23** continue to roll out waves of joy. Confidence, creativity, and even romance can rise to greater heights when Mercury enters your entertaining 5th House on **September 25**, followed by the Libra New Moon on **September 27**. There may be a price to pay, however, since domineering Pluto forms a stressful square to the New Moon. You could be forced to make a difficult choice when warm Venus joins cold Saturn on **September 29**, closing one path toward pleasure in order to keep another one open.

SEPTEMBER 2011

THURSDAY 1	
FRIDAY 2	
SATURDAY 3	
SUNDAY 4	
MONDAY 5	
TUESDAY 6	
WEDNESDAY 7	

THURSDAY 8 ★ Objectivity chases away illusions

FRIDAY 9 ★	
SATURDAY 10	
SUNDAY 11	

MONDAY 12 ★ ○ **SUPER NOVA DAYS** Ask your colleagues for help

TUESDAY 13 ★	
WEDNESDAY 14 ★	
THURSDAY 15	
FRIDAY 16	
SATURDAY 17	
SUNDAY 18	
MONDAY 19	
TUESDAY 20	
WEDNESDAY 21	

THURSDAY 22 ★ Mixed messages throw off your perceptions

FRIDAY 23 ★	
SATURDAY 24 ★	
SUNDAY 25 ★	
MONDAY 26	

TUESDAY 27 ★ ● You can't control other people's thoughts

WEDNESDAY 28 ★	
THURSDAY 29	
FRIDAY 30	

GEMINI OCTOBER 2011 OVERVIEW

THE ART OF REGENERATION

Responsibility forces its stern hand onto your playground this month, interrupting the fun to remind you not to spend time frivolously. The games, distractions, and flirtations that keep your naturally curious mind happily entertained run into walls of resistance on several fronts. Stylish Venus is the first to leave the party when she says goodbye to your lighthearted 5th House on **October 9**. Turn your intensity toward your job, because the love planet then enters Scorpio and your 6th House of Work. Finding a deeper level of motivation and developing your skills could eventually earn you more recognition and fulfillment. On **October 11**, the Full Moon in energizing Aries falls in your 11th House of Groups and Friends, which usually spurs new activity in your social life. However, this one is shadowed by somber Saturn's conjunction to the Sun and opposition to the Moon; elf-doubt or external restrictions may diminish your optimism.

The Sun's move into passionate Scorpio and your 6th House on **October 23** underscores the pressing demands of your daily life. Still, you may see some light at the end of the tunnel on **October 26**, when upbeat Jupiter in your 12th House of Spirituality and Dreams opposes the intense Scorpio New Moon. While others operate in a dog-eat-dog world of limited resources, you may be tapping into a well of boundless faith and imagination that counters their fears. Growth arising from loss is a powerful theme expressed through Jupiter's harmonious trine to transformational Pluto on **October 28**, the second in a series that began on **July 7** and ends on **March 13, 2012**.

OCTOBER 2011

SATURDAY 1	
SUNDAY 2	
MONDAY 3	
TUESDAY 4	
WEDNESDAY 5	
THURSDAY 6 ★	Find the information you need and commit it to memory
FRIDAY 7	
SATURDAY 8	
SUNDAY 9	
MONDAY 10	
TUESDAY 11 ★	○ Follow your own star
WEDNESDAY 12 ★	
THURSDAY 13 ★	
FRIDAY 14	
SATURDAY 15	
SUNDAY 16 ★	Be alert to an overdose of optimism
MONDAY 17 ★	
TUESDAY 18	
WEDNESDAY 19	
THURSDAY 20	
FRIDAY 21	
SATURDAY 22	
SUNDAY 23 ★	Apply unconventional ideas to your work
MONDAY 24 ★	
TUESDAY 25	
WEDNESDAY 26 ★	● SUPER NOVA DAYS Transform your fear into passion
THURSDAY 27 ★	
FRIDAY 28 ★	
SATURDAY 29	
SUNDAY 30	
MONDAY 31	

GEMINI NOVEMBER 2011 OVERVIEW

TRAFFIC MANAGEMENT

Your enthusiasm for connecting with people could create problems this month. Vivacious Venus and chatty Mercury enter risk-taking Sagittarius and your 7th House of Others on **November 2**, increasing your opportunities for making new contacts. Personal and business alliances seem especially alluring when potential partners are so optimistic and generous. However, you must turn your attention to domestic issues with Mars's move into your 4th House of Home and Family on **November 10**. The Taurus Full Moon on the same day falls in your 12th House of Escapism, drawing you away from public projects and directing your thoughts to private needs and spiritual matters.

The Sun firing into extroverted Sagittarius and your 7th House on **November 22** puts more wind in your social sails, yet Mercury's retrograde turn on **November 24** sends a very different message. Your ruling planet has been slowing down in advance of this change of direction, which makes it harder to assimilate new data and experiences. You're tempted to overstuff your mind with Mercury in opinionated Sagittarius, leaving lots of loose ends. The usual communication complications of Mercury retrograde, lasting until **December 13**, could be extended this time around. The strongest evidence that something may be amiss in your relationships is the Sagittarius New Moon in your 7th House on **November 25**. This lunation is a Solar Eclipse with hard aspects to Mars, Neptune, and Jupiter—a complex combination warning you not to expect too much of others. Any gains that you make in partnerships now only come if you exercise caution and self-control.

NOVEMBER 2011

TUESDAY 1 ★ Your dreams can inspire others

WEDNESDAY 2 ★
THURSDAY 3 ★
FRIDAY 4
SATURDAY 5
SUNDAY 6
MONDAY 7
TUESDAY 8
WEDNESDAY 9
THURSDAY 10 ★ ○ Be practical without losing touch with your soul's needs

---

FRIDAY 11
SATURDAY 12
SUNDAY 13
MONDAY 14
TUESDAY 15
WEDNESDAY 16 ★ Don't let logic get in the way of your instincts

---

THURSDAY 17 ★
FRIDAY 18 ★
SATURDAY 19
SUNDAY 20
MONDAY 21
TUESDAY 22
WEDNESDAY 23 ★ **SUPER NOVA DAYS** Delays can feel like major setbacks

---

THURSDAY 24 ★
FRIDAY 25 ★ ●
SATURDAY 26
SUNDAY 27
MONDAY 28
TUESDAY 29
WEDNESDAY 30

GEMINI DECEMBER 2011 OVERVIEW

SAY GOOD-BYE TO YESTERDAY

Your year ends, Gemini, with a long look back that can change your view of the past and reduce its influence on your life. The key event is a Lunar Eclipse in Gemini on **December 10** that's bound to cause some serious soul searching. You may be tempted to talk your feelings away instead of facing them, but the message is clear: Let go of an old story about yourself that keeps you turning in circles. Mercury is retrograde until **December 13**, encouraging you to use this month as a time of review. Pay close attention to relationship patterns that are tying you up in knots with this backward cycle in your 7th House of Partnerships. Mercury's conjunction with your Sun on **December 4** can plant seeds of inspiration that let you write a new script for a happier future.

Tantalizing Venus's entry into innovative Aquarius and your 9th House of Higher Truth on **December 20** is a strong magnet pulling you toward experimentation and away from the values of your childhood. Travel, education, or smart strangers can show you a world of exotic experiences and liberating ideas to satisfy your ever-curious mind. A wise mentor or reliable ally helps you build a foundation to support this new reality when the Sun's entry into ambitious Capricorn and your resource-rich 8th House marks the Winter Solstice on **December 22**. The Capricorn New Moon on **December 24** tests your commitment with its conjunction to Pluto. This tiny but potent planet will show you the price of reaching for higher goals or taking a relationship to the next level. The cost may be great, but the rewards should be even greater.

DECEMBER 2011

THURSDAY 1 ★ Impatience could lead to harsh words

FRIDAY 2 ★
SATURDAY 3 ★
SUNDAY 4 ★
MONDAY 5
TUESDAY 6
WEDNESDAY 7
THURSDAY 8
FRIDAY 9
SATURDAY 10 ★ ○ **SUPER NOVA DAYS** Acting decisively creates momentum

SUNDAY 11 ★
MONDAY 12
TUESDAY 13 ★ Move ahead with potential new contacts

WEDNESDAY 14
THURSDAY 15
FRIDAY 16
SATURDAY 17
SUNDAY 18
MONDAY 19
TUESDAY 20
WEDNESDAY 21
THURSDAY 22 ★ Toss caution to the wind

FRIDAY 23
SATURDAY 24 ●
SUNDAY 25
MONDAY 26
TUESDAY 27
WEDNESDAY 28 ★ Too much information stretches your nerves

THURSDAY 29 ★
FRIDAY 30
SATURDAY 31

2012 HOROSCOPE

GEMINI

MAY 21–JUNE 20

GEMINI

OVERVIEW OF THE YEAR

This could be a great year for you because bountiful Jupiter returns to your sign on June 11 for its once-every-twelve-year visit. You might grow impatient waiting for Jupiter to enter clever Gemini, but there's much to do in preparation for the opportunities awaiting you. **It would be wise to use the first part of the year to finish up old business** while Jupiter moves through your 12th House of Endings. You are being given a chance to see how previous successes and failures are connected to recurring patterns in your life. You can fine-tune your current ambitions with the insights you gain, empowering you to plan for the future with newfound confidence.

Once the giant planet reaches your 1st House of Self on June 11, it's important to take your own counsel and trust yourself, rather than allowing the opinions of others to carry too much weight. Jupiter is astrology's most fortunate planet, and its yearlong visit to your sign is a harbinger of the significant personal growth in front of you. **This is not about achieving overnight success;**

nevertheless, a positive attitude can lead to advancement in business and growing public recognition. Even if a decision turns out to be a mistake, you are able to quickly learn from it and adjust your course accordingly. This is not a time to stand still, but rather a calling to set high goals in all areas of your life and then reach for the stars.

Although you can make a lot of progress this year, it becomes more challenging to be realistic about your life purpose when spiritual Neptune enters your 10th House of Public Responsibility on February 3. This long-lasting transit can inspire you to seek more meaning from your work, yet it also complicates your professional aspirations if being of service becomes more important than making money. A lack of clarity about your goals could tempt you to stretch too far or miss your mark entirely when boundless Jupiter squares confusing Neptune on June 25. But uncertainty will likely be swept away by the opening act of a larger-than-life drama activated by the first of seven Uranus-Pluto squares on June 24. This dynamic conflict between independent Uranus in your 11th House of Long-Term Goals and intense Pluto in your 8th House of Intimacy can raise questions

OVERVIEW OF THE YEAR

about who's in control of your life. **You may need to reevaluate your priorities and take bold action to establish new objectives.** Personal and professional relationships are stressed when you make sudden changes that profoundly impact others as well as yourself. Fortunately, the issues emphasized this year won't require a final resolution until the last Uranus-Pluto square in 2015. Still, it's wise to start working on a major overhaul of your goals now, while the planets are still working in your favor.

GEMINI 2012

KEEP IT REAL

Karmic Saturn in relationship-oriented Libra and your 5th House of Love anchors you to the status quo until October 5, and it's important that you continue to work on existing issues. On June 4, the cavalier Sagittarius Full Moon Eclipse rattles your 7th House of Partnerships. Its opposition to sweet Venus and square to combative Mars can reignite painful feelings. If you don't face serious matters of contention with a loved one, the restless Gemini New Moon Eclipse on June 19 could lead to foolish actions that you might later regret. Your relationship houses are activated again by the Gemini Full Moon Eclipse on November 28, but its conjunction with beneficial Jupiter suggests a positive outcome as long as you keep channels of communication open throughout the year.

OVERVIEW OF THE YEAR

WHAT DREAMS ARE MADE OF

It's difficult to maintain a balanced perspective about your professional life when giant Jupiter clashes with fuzzy Neptune on June 25 and maverick Chiron on July 24. However, if you don't over-inflate your expectations, your dreams can inspire you to great heights. With compassionate Neptune camped out in your 10th House of Career until 2025, you'll need to realign your objectives with a higher calling. You should receive much-needed assistance from dependable Saturn's entry into your 6th House of Employment on October 5. Turn your fantasies into reality and overcome self-imposed limitations when stabilizing Saturn trines Neptune and Chiron on October 10 and November 16.

GEMINI 2012

UPS AND DOWNS

Your income and spending patterns fluctuate with your emotions throughout the year. Applying yourself with steady determination could bring rewards, however, especially on March 13–14 as Venus joins opulent Jupiter and trines Pluto and Mars to create a beneficial Grand Earth Trine. Don't fritter away your gains when Venus turns retrograde in your sign on May 15–June 27. Be especially careful about making a risky investment around the Full Moon Eclipse on June 4. Money matters generally improve when Venus visits your 2nd House of Income on August 7–September 6, with the exception of a rough spot on August 15–16. Be confident about a financial decision on October 9, but don't overextend yourself. Unexpected financial wrinkles on November 1–3 should smooth out by November 9.

OVERVIEW OF THE YEAR

PROACTIVE MEASURES

Unexpressed emotions can have a significant impact on your physical condition this year as volcanic Pluto squares uncontrollable Uranus on June 24 and September 19. Stand strong and make healthy lifestyle changes early in the year, for the South Lunar Node is in Gemini through August 29, encouraging your tendency to adapt to stress by dancing around its edges rather than dealing with the real issues. Fortunately, Mars in your 6th House of Health on August 23–October 6 boosts your vitality, but you must express excess energy rather than turning it inward. Strict Saturn points out your physical weak spots; only extra effort on your part will protect your health when it enters your 6th House on October 5 for a two-year visit. The mysterious Scorpio Solar Eclipse on November 13 brings a secret out into the open. Although this might be temporarily upsetting, it should ultimately have a positive effect on your health by releasing detrimental tension.

HOME IS WHERE YOUR HEART IS

A change of address isn't out of the question this year, but you'll experience an intense focus on domestic affairs even if you don't move anywhere. Assertive Mars in your 4th House of Home and Family until July 3 motivates you to take a stand for what you want. But Mars is retrograde on January 23–April 13, provoking irritability and even conflict. It's a smart idea to burn off excess heat now by undertaking physically demanding projects around the house or in the garden. Your family is in the spotlight when the Sun and Mercury make their yearly visits to your 4th House on August 22–September 22. Finally, domestic issues settle down on October 3–28 when lovely Venus passes through your 4th House. Take time to enjoy a peaceful interlude and relax with those you love.

OVERVIEW OF THE YEAR

WANDERLUST

You may have big plans for traveling this year, but turning them into reality could take time. Although your 9th House of Voyages is activated by covetous Venus until January 14, her conjunction with imaginative Neptune on the 13th is what stimulates your dreams of faraway lands. The Sun and Mercury further illuminate your travel plans on January 20–February 19, but you are wiser to wait for liftoff until after journeying Jupiter enters Gemini on June 11. You may be less interested in short business trips or quick weekend getaways now, for you see yourself on a bigger quest. You are attracted to exotic places that expand your mind and deepen your sense of meaning. Pay extra attention to details and confirm your reservations twice if you need to travel when Mercury is retrograde on March 12–April 4, July 14–August 8, and November 6–26.

GEMINI 2012

SPIRITUAL WARRIOR

You began a quest to rediscover the purpose of your life when philosophical Jupiter entered practical Taurus and your 12th House of Soul Consciousness on June 11, 2011. Jupiter remains in this mysterious house until June 11, 2012, motivating you to continue your metaphysical studies or to find a spiritual teacher or guru. And although all journeys begin with a first step, you cannot rest upon what you learn. It's time to project your inner experiences onto the outer world—and fortunately metaphysical Neptune enters your 10th House of Public Responsibility on February 3 for a fourteen-year stay to help with this process.

RICK & JEFF'S TIP FOR THE YEAR
Maintain a Healthy Perspective

The rate of change is escalating and you may feel pressure to make decisions that will have a lasting impact. Events can pile up so quickly that you lose your objectivity. Blind optimism and extreme pessimism are not helpful, yet may be the result from having no clear frame of reference. Unquestionably, these are times of great transition, but they, too, will fade into the past. Avoid the shortsighted desperation that comes from fear by remembering to look out beyond the present moment and toward the distant horizon.

JANUARY

JANUARY

ON THE THRESHOLD OF A DREAM

The future seems so close this month that you might just want to reach out to grab it. Unfortunately, even if you're sure a goal is right around the corner, you might actually need all year to reach it. That's because hardworking Saturn edges closer all year to a harmonious trine with inspirational Neptune in your 11th House of Dreams, but doesn't actually get there until **October 10**. On **January 7**, your key planet, Mercury, forms supportive sextiles to both Saturn and Neptune, coaxing you to believe that your fantasies are real. Mental Mercury's entry into calculating Capricorn and your 8th House of Shared Resources on **January 8** enables you to be more practical by involving others in your plans. Although you can incorporate their ambitions into your overall strategy, the tenacious Cancer Full Moon on **January 9** illuminates your 2nd House of Personal Resources, shifting the focus back to your individual needs.

You may find the recognition that you seek with Venus's move into your 10th House of Career on **January 14**—if you remain focused on your objectives. You'll need self-discipline when the ambitious Capricorn Sun squares scrupulous Saturn on **January 19**. But resistance falls away as the Sun enters experimental Aquarius and your 9th House of Big Ideas on **January 20** and squares expansive Jupiter on **January 22**. Your progress could slow as energetic Mars turns retrograde on **January 23**, the same day as the futuristic Aquarius New Moon. Even if your tactics are sound and your execution is skillful, you still might feel as if you're losing ground. Don't panic; Mercury enters Aquarius and your visionary 9th House on **January 27**, stimulating innovative thinking as you reformulate your plans.

KEEP IN MIND THIS MONTH

Success doesn't necessarily look the way you expect. Although you might be disappointed, what you do now can be instrumental in what you accomplish later on in the year.

JANUARY ♊

KEY DATES

★ JANUARY 1
ears wide open

You'd like to enjoy this day off with your friends and family, but you might become irritable if holiday festivities don't meet your expectations. You think that you're being reasonable, but if others don't agree they will tell you exactly where your logic has gone astray. Instead of reacting defensively, listen to the feedback you receive now because it could help you in the days ahead.

SUPER NOVA DAYS

★ JANUARY 7-9
trust your intuition

Your thinking is sound on **January 7** when intelligent Mercury connects with authoritative Saturn and psychic Neptune. Be prepared to make your plans even more concrete when Mercury enters earthy Capricorn the next day. But if Mercury's easy trine to opinionated Jupiter encourages false assumptions, its harsh square to electric Uranus can shock you with the truth. Ultimately, what you choose is not as important as honoring your own feelings, for the sensitive Cancer Full Moon on **January 9** falls in your 2nd House of Values, gently reminding you not to abandon your core beliefs.

★ **JANUARY 12-13**
in the zone
Harmonious aspects to uncontainable Mars on the **12th** and taskmaster Saturn on the **13th** motivate you to roll up your sleeves and work extra-hard. Fortunately, your efforts should be rewarded, because you know what you want and are willing to be patient in order to achieve the desired results. But clever Mercury joins potent Pluto in your 8th House of Transformation, enticing you to believe that you have superpowers and can get whatever you want. Be careful about pushing your agenda too hard or you could undo your recent gains.

★ **JANUARY 21-23**
slow down; you're moving too fast
You may not be very efficient in the days prior to the intelligent Aquarius New Moon in your

JANUARY ♊

9th House of Journeys on **January 23** as you think about the great adventures ahead. The Aquarius Sun is zapped by Uranus the Awakener on **January 21**, blasting your brain with inventive ideas. The Sun's dynamic square to global Jupiter on the **22nd** extends your vision even farther. But the winged messenger Mercury trines Mars just as the warrior planet turns retrograde on the **23rd**. Although this could unravel your plans, it also can extend a deadline, giving you more time to get everything in order.

★ **JANUARY 27–28**
blue skies ahead
A somber Mercury-Saturn square on **January 27** can bring discouragement as a setback reveals a flaw in your plan. Fortunately, Mercury combines with brilliant Uranus and broad-minded Jupiter on the **28th**, enabling you to come up with bright ideas to overcome almost any obstacle in your path.

FEBRUARY

FEBRUARY

VISION QUEST

This month gets off to a bumpy start with relationship issues affecting your ability to concentrate at work, but the overall outlook is still relatively smooth. Angry words may slip off your tongue too easily on **February 1**, when communicator Mercury forms an anxious aspect with argumentative Mars. But if you're careful about what you say when Mercury creates tension on **February 6**, **9–10**, **and 23–25**, the little flare-ups that might occur won't be obstacles to your happiness or success. You may sense a subtle yet profound shift of energy when slow-moving Neptune the Dreamer swims into watery Pisces and your 10th House of Career on **February 3** for a thirteen-year stay. You could become disillusioned with your chosen life path, dreaming about changing your occupation to a more meaningful pursuit. Talking about your dissatisfaction can lead to constructive feedback when Mercury trines trustworthy Saturn on **February 13**. Your dreams inspire you to reach beyond the ordinary as Mercury conjuncts Neptune on the **14th**, followed by the Sun on the **19th**.

GEMINI 2012

You may feel a powerful urge to share an original idea on **February 7**, when the expressive Leo Full Moon brightens your 3rd House of Information and Education. Eloquent Mercury is aligned with the Sun in intellectual Aquarius, allowing the words to flow like quicksilver. But your aspirations may take longer to reach fruition than you realize, because Saturn the Tester turns retrograde in your 5th House of Self-Expression just hours prior to the Full Moon. Harsh criticism or stubborn resistance to your professional plans won't deter you on **February 21**, when the imaginative Pisces New Moon joins visionary Neptune in your 10th House of Responsibility.

KEEP IN MIND THIS MONTH

Even if you have to handle one concern after another, minor interruptions won't get in the way of your long-term progress.

FEBRUARY ♊

KEY DATES

★ **FEBRUARY 1**
cosmic tug-of-war
You can feel the dissension in the air as the cosmic lovers, Venus and Mars, pull in opposite directions. Enticing Venus in your professional 10th House can turn the workplace into a playground, luring you away from home. You may already be short-tempered with cranky Mars now retrograde in your 4th House of Domestic Conditions, so quarrelsome Mercury could incite conflict as it stressfully aspects Mars. Although the tension is palpable, don't succumb to your frustration and start an unnecessary fight.

SUPER NOVA DAYS

★ **FEBRUARY 7-10**
call of the wild
You are inspired to do things differently this week, and the demonstrative Leo Full Moon on **February 7** can bring your ideas into bloom. The Sun's alignment with persuasive Mercury in your 9th House of Future Vision gives you

the passion you need to convince others that you are speaking the truth. But needy Venus forms an annoying quincunx with doubting Saturn, possibly inhibiting others from fully supporting you. Luckily, Venus enters pioneering Aries on the **8th** and joins explosive Uranus on the **9th**, creating the breakthrough you desire. Nevertheless, your excitement still may be tempered by a controlling Mercury-Pluto aspect on **February 10**, indicating that a powerful person might resist your suggestion and hinder your progress.

★ **FEBRUARY 14–18**
dare to believe
Your Valentine's Day expectations are high thanks to Mercury's dreamy conjunction with wistful Neptune on **February 14**, but if the power equation is out of balance you may see the darker side of love with a tough square between romantic Venus and passionate Pluto the next day. A struggle for control could get out of hand, but calm communication should smooth ruffled feathers when Mercury sextiles cheerful Jupiter on the

FEBRUARY

16th and Pluto on the **18th**. Luckily, the Sun's superconductive trine to responsible Saturn assures that your good judgment will prevail.

★ FEBRUARY 21–23
account for your actions
The Pisces New Moon on **February 21** affirms the current emphasis on your 10th House of Public Responsibility, yet you may struggle to see your objectives due to the presence of misleading Neptune. If the awkward Venus-Mars quincunx on **February 22** tricks you into making a social faux pas, apologize and move on. Defending bad behavior, even if inadvertent, will just escalate the problem when Mercury opposes impertinent Mars on **February 23**.

★ FEBRUARY 28
all's well that ends well
You are at the top of your game today as the Sun in your 10th House of Status sextiles insightful Pluto. Instead of spending time reviewing the past, concentrate on the present moment; your well-intended actions should have positive results.

MARCH

MARCH ♊

BUILDING A FOUNDATION

It's hard to relax because you're so excited about what's ahead, and your impatience is nearly unbearable with Mercury blasting into impetuous Aries on **March 2**. But a series of tense aspects to Mars in your 4th House of Family and Saturn in your 5th House of Spontaneity on **March 2–4** can block your progress by weighing you down with personal matters or parental responsibilities. Although fleet-footed Mercury usually speeds up your thought process while in Aries, you may feel mentally sluggish as the messenger planet slows to enter its retrograde phase on **March 12**. Now that both Mars and Mercury are traveling backward, you may find that these two planets can place a hold on an important project or indicate unexpected delays, especially if you feel pressure to make something happen right now. Paradoxically, when your momentum is interrupted or a deadline is postponed, you may actually feel a sense of relief—as if you've been graced with additional time to get your plans in order.

You find much-needed calm amid a sea of change when the analytical Virgo Full Moon on

GEMINI 2012

March 8 highlights your domestic 4th House and activates a practical Grand Earth Trine. Although this grand trine peaks on **March 13–14**, giving you an overall sense of well-being, it is no time to be lazy. What you do now can have a profound and lasting impact, even if success seems postponed. Another wave of enthusiasm ensues at the Spring Equinox on **March 20** when the Sun enters fiery Aries to light up your 11th House of Goals. But even if you have accepted the lingering constraints to progress, the enterprising Aries New Moon on **March 22** kicks off the next cycle and focuses your attention on the future.

KEEP IN MIND THIS MONTH

Don't expect too much too soon from your current investments of time or money. Frustration and disappointment could get in the way of your success.

MARCH

KEY DATES

★ **MARCH 1–3**
shoulder to the wheel
You feel like a pinball being bounced around when your words run into a judgmental Mercury-Saturn quincunx on **March 1**. But you aren't willing to take no for an answer when quicksilver Mercury enters excitable Aries on **March 2**. You may be surprised that your enthusiasm doesn't carry you farther, but ambitious Saturn's harsh aspects to Mars and the Sun will demand more hard work from you before you can achieve success. The Sun in your 10th House of Status tensely opposes militant Mars on the **3rd**, indicating that you may need to fight for what you deserve. Pick your battles wisely or you'll lose ground by alienating those who can help you reach your goals.

★ **MARCH 5**
stroke of genius
You're hit with lightning bolts of original ideas and out-of-the-blue solutions to irresolvable

problems today thanks to quick-witted Mercury's conjunction with electrifying Uranus. It can be difficult for you to remember your thoughts, they come and go so quickly. Normally, this cerebral activation occurs annually, but Mercury's retrograde will reactivate this innovative aspect on **March 18**, so you have a second chance this month to turn your brainstorm into reality.

SUPER NOVA DAYS

★ **MARCH 12-14**
lucky break
Although Mercury turns retrograde on **March 12**, its three-week reversal is softened by a Grand Earth Trine that stabilizes your life against the uncontrollable changing tides. This grand trine rests upon the powerful connection between confident Jupiter and fierce Pluto that is exact on **March 13**. Unfortunately, the sweet presence of delicious Venus can be so comforting that you don't take advantage of the energy now at your disposal. The auspicious Venus-Jupiter conjunction on **March 14** falls in your 12th House of Destiny,

MARCH

indicating a possible financial windfall or luck in love. The third point of this magical grand trine is held by retrograde Mars in your 4th House of Security, reinforcing your drive for satisfaction in your personal, rather than professional, life.

★ **MARCH 26-29**
navigating rough waters
Mischievous Mercury retrogrades through tricky territory in your 10th House of Career. On **March 26** you may be reminded of Murphy's Law: "If anything can go wrong, it will." Fortunately, the Winged Messenger aspects buoyant Jupiter soon after restrictive Saturn, so snafus at work shouldn't last long. Meanwhile, a transformative Saturn-Pluto quintile on the **28th** requires you to reconsider your entire strategy, and an intensifying Sun-Pluto square on **March 29** fuels a conflict if you aren't willing to modify your long-term goals.

APRIL

APRIL

ON THE MOVE

This month, your recent efforts begin to bring you the acknowledgment and financial rewards you seek. Venus, the planet of love and money, enters your sign on **April 3**, initiating a feel-good period when you find it easier to attract positive attention. Normally, this phase lasts for only a few weeks, but Venus turns retrograde on **May 15**, extending her visit until **August 7**. Although the overall effects of this transit should be pleasurable, Venus squares whimsical Neptune on **April 5** and physical Mars on **April 7**, creating stress associated with your unfulfilled desires. Fortunately, unexpected gratification is possible when Venus sextiles surprising Uranus on **April 9**. Meanwhile, communicator Mercury—retrograding since **March 12**—turns direct in your 10th House of Career on **April 4** to free up blockages in your professional plans. Pent-up tensions begin to dissipate on **April 13** when Mars finishes his retrograde phase, which started on **January 23**. An additional boost of energy increases your momentum, although it may take a few days for you to notice the effect.

GEMINI 2012

You'll likely feel overwhelmed when the sociable Libra Full Moon shines the spotlight on your 5th House of Love on **April 6**, forming harsh aspects with Venus, Mars, and Neptune and further intensifying a relationship dilemma. The steadfast Taurus New Moon in your 12th House of Inner Peace on **April 21** is a welcome relief from the hectic pace of life. Its harmonious aspects to Mars and Neptune come to the rescue and give you an opportunity to put your feet up, indulge your senses, and relax. Enjoy yourself now while you have the chance.

KEEP IN MIND THIS MONTH

It's smart to recharge your batteries as the stress subsides—but be sure you don't frivolously waste an opportunity to improve your life.

APRIL ♊

KEY DATES

★ APRIL 4–7
green light

Be ready to jump if you receive the go-ahead on a work project that recently encountered delays as your ruling planet, Mercury, turns direct on **April 4**. Luckily, a powerful quintile between flamboyant Jupiter and fanciful Neptune enables you to be even more creative than usual. But be careful, because flirty Venus in fickle Gemini squares deceptive Neptune on **April 5**; you're so convincing, you could even fool yourself. The lovely Libra Full Moon on **April 6** increases your ability to please others, but a Venus-Mars square on **April 7** leads to trouble if you aren't being completely honest with everyone involved.

★ APRIL 12–16
uphill climb

Witty Mercury cannot help you talk your way out of a tight spot on **April 12** when it forms an uncomfortable quincunx to severe Saturn. Unfortunately, the Sun's tense opposition to

Saturn on **April 15** is even more judgmental and less forgiving. But you're not eager to succumb to the voice of authority when sizzling Mars turns up the heat by going direct on **April 13**, followed by Mercury's entry into red-hot Aries on the **16th**. Hard work, rather than clever words, is your current key to success.

SUPER NOVA DAYS

★ APRIL 20-23
irreconcilable differences
You can't anticipate the impact of what you say when loquacious Mercury in Aries quincunxes Mars on **April 20**. Your crazy ideas may trigger unexpected anger, especially when Mercury hooks up with unstable Uranus on the **22nd**. Fortunately, Mars is sweetly trined by sensible Taurus New Moon on the **21st** and by the Sun on the **23rd**, enabling you to defend your innovative ideas against a senseless attack.

★ APRIL 25
the truth shall set you free
You are being challenged today to dig beneath the surface until you know the score, and then

you must share what you learn. Paradoxically, expressive Mercury's square to ruthless Pluto demonstrates the messenger planet's power to overcome dark forces by exposing hidden information. Your openness and integrity prove that fear is no match for the truth.

★ APRIL 29
destiny's calling

An unstoppable wave of change washes through your life now as the solidifying Taurus Sun in your 12th House of Spirituality forms a superconductive trine to transformational Pluto. Normally, you would be tempted to avoid this level of intensity, but you intuitively know there's no way around it. There are aspects of your life that aren't working, yet you've been unable to let them go. Rather than being frightened by the unknown territory ahead, you are eager to explore it, for you know this is your chance to advance and evolve.

MAY

MAY ♊

SLOW DOWN AND SMELL THE ROSES

Conflicting cosmic messages rev up your communication engine while also tempting you with the peace and quiet of increased isolation. Paradoxically, your friends are even more important to you than usual, as this month begins with chatty Mercury in excitable Aries in your 11th House Social Networking. But your quick wit isn't a substitute for real understanding, and Mercury's worried opposition to judgmental Saturn on **May 5**—the same day as the intense Scorpio Full Moon—reminds you that others may not be entertained by your lighthearted humor. Mercury's entry into easygoing Taurus and your 12th House of Privacy on **May 9** is another sign that you need to slow down and maybe even retreat into a more relaxed lifestyle for a while. Fewer distractions are in order while three planets—Mercury, the Sun, and Jupiter—travel through your secretive 12th House.

Pleasure-seeking Venus turns retrograde in your sign on **May 15**, highlighting your need for reflection and solitude. Nevertheless, she remains in your

GEMINI 2012

1st House of Personality for an extended stay until **August 7**, offering her blessings of love and money to those who are patient. But waiting isn't your forte, and the Sun's entry into flighty Gemini on **May 20**, just a few hours prior to a Solar Eclipse, can make you anxious. However, this New Moon Eclipse is also a start of a fresh cycle if you're willing to let go of your old expectations. The pace of your life quickens when your ruling planet, Mercury, flies into noisy Gemini on **May 24**.

KEEP IN MIND THIS MONTH

Although your life is settling into a steady rhythm, be prepared to revise your plans when the tempo shifts.

MAY ♊

KEY DATES

★ **MAY 5–7**
bigger is better
You seek ways to better yourself on **May 5**, when the complex Scorpio Full Moon illuminates your 6th House of Self-Improvement. However, you may be overwhelmed by how much you want to change; it's hard to know where to start. You have no shortage of good ideas, but they are dismissed by people who question your ability as your key planet, Mercury, opposes stern Saturn. Baby steps won't work now. Take a leap of faith; grandiose Jupiter aspects radical Uranus on **May 7**, rewarding bold and innovative action.

★ **MAY 13–16**
beyond the horizon
The Sun's annual conjunction with jaunty Jupiter on **May 13** fills you with confidence. Luckily, you intuitively know how to translate an opportunity into reality now as articulate Mercury in reliable Taurus forms a solid Grand Earth Trine with courageous Mars and

formidable Pluto on **May 13–16**. You can draw on deep reserves of energy to accomplish your goals, but you still may fall short of your own high expectations because Jupiter forms an irritating quincunx with pessimistic Saturn on **May 16**. Additionally, Venus begins her six-week retrograde phase on **May 15**, tempting you with the promise of satisfaction while placing it just beyond your reach. Don't let frustration get the best of you; use your time wisely by preparing for what's ahead.

SUPER NOVA DAYS

★ **MAY 20–22**
let the new times roll
You know better than to hold on to your past when the Sun and Moon enter restless Gemini on **May 20** and the New Moon Eclipse pushes the restart button in your 1st House of Self. This Solar Eclipse forms an imaginative biquintile to productive Saturn in your 5th House of Self-Expression, enabling you to tap into a creative flow. But managing the intensity can challenge you, especially with verbal Mercury forming uneasy aspects with Saturn

and Pluto on **May 21**. Although you may think that an idea is not worth pursuing, Mercury's conjunction with promising Jupiter on the **22nd** restores your confidence in your plan and encourages you to take it to the next level.

★ MAY 27–30
hot under the collar

Your innovative thoughts are not restrained by social etiquette when expressive Mercury joins the Sun in curious Gemini. Together, on **May 27–28**, this pair creates a cooperative sextile with unorthodox Uranus in your 11th House of Groups, inviting you to share your radical ideas with friends. Unfortunately, they may not be as supportive as you wish. Be cautious; Mercury's square to competitive Mars on **May 30** can reveal differences of opinion that escalate into an unnecessary argument.

JUNE

JUNE

OPPORTUNITY KNOCKS

Every twelve years, expansive Jupiter visits your sign for a year, bearing good news and initiating another cycle of opportunity. Your self-confidence soars as this gassy giant begins pumping up your 1st House of Self on **June 11**. But this month becomes a dance between optimistic hopes and unrealistic dreams, because Jupiter slowly moves toward a disquieting square with mythical Neptune that culminates on **June 25**, challenging you to keep your expectations in perspective. Meanwhile, an unexpected clash over money could erupt between you and your friends or associates when volatile Uranus in your 11th House of Groups squares relentless Pluto in your 8th House of Shared Resources on **June 24**. Someone may exert power over you through manipulative behavior such as withholding money or love, precipitating unexpected events that are beyond your control. Fortunately, this is only the opening volley; you have time to figure out how to handle the next round of conflict, as the Uranus-Pluto square recurs seven times through **March 16, 2015**.

GEMINI 2012

A business or personal relationship brings excitement into your life on **June 4**, when the Sagittarius Full Moon Eclipse falls in your 7th House of Partnerships. Step back and contemplate your feelings when your key planet, Mercury, slips out of your sign and into introspective Cancer on **June 7**. The Gemini New Moon on **June 19** is your time to make a fresh start, yet it's so close to the Summer Solstice on **June 20** that you may lack objectivity as you move closer to the great changes ahead. Luckily, you are able to express yourself more decisively when cerebral Mercury enters lively Leo and your 3rd House of Information on **June 25**.

KEEP IN MIND THIS MONTH

This is a bellwether month that can give you a glimpse of the dynamic landscape you'll be traversing over the next few years.

JUNE ♊

KEY DATES

★ **JUNE 3–5**
fairy-tale ending
You're finally ready to settle down and take yourself seriously when thoughtful Mercury forms a productive trine to sobering Saturn on **June 3**. However, it's nearly impossible to maintain a rational approach to your responsibilities while also responding to the stresses of a personal relationship. The adventurous Sagittarius Lunar Eclipse on **June 4** distracts you with visions of distant horizons. But its alignment with retrograde Venus in flirtatious Gemini and square to aggressive Mars can turn the heat up on love too much and too fast unless you pay close attention to your emotions. Fortunately, Venus conjoins the Sun on **June 5**, indicating a pleasant outcome to a challenging series of events.

★ **JUNE 11–13**
patience, grasshopper
Although you may be inspired by the arrival of jolly Jupiter in your sign on **June 11**,

you're also distracted as nervous Mercury squares erratic Uranus and opposes Pluto, foreshadowing the Uranus-Pluto square that's exact on **June 24**. An unexpected change in your financial condition is possible with Mercury in your 2nd House of Self-Worth, but the current tension might also stem from a power play in a complicated relationship. Self-restraint is advised; wait to make your move until clarity returns when the Sun trines stabilizing Saturn on **June 13**.

★ **JUNE 19–21**
start from scratch
Your current restlessness reaches a tipping point at the Gemini New Moon on **June 19**. However, it's unlikely that you'll make any significant changes yet because the Sun slips into passive Cancer on **June 20**, turning your energy inward and slowing your pace. Additionally, you may need to confront the shortcomings of your escape plan as the frustrating Mercury-Saturn square unravels your dreams, crashing them down to earth. But all is not lost, for a thrilling Venus-Uranus

JUNE ♊

sextile dangles new carrots of desire in front of you and you receive an energetic boost on **June 21**, when Mercury forms an opportunistic sextile with go-getter Mars.

SUPER NOVA DAYS

★ **JUNE 27–29**

stormy weather

Changes are coming fast and furious now. If you made good use of Venus's retrograde period—it began on **May 15**—her direct turn on **June 27** begins a process that can bring greater freedom of expression and financial rewards for your efforts. But first you must navigate through the troubled waters stirred by the Sun's opposition to secretive Pluto and square to rebellious Uranus on **June 29**. Remember, issues around money, control, and personal relationships may be overwhelming you in the moment, but they're tied to longer-lasting cycles that will continue to have significant impact.

JULY

JULY ♊

ADJUSTING TO A NEW REALITY

Although the changes that began recently could take months, even years, to play through to their conclusions, there's no doubt that you have entered a new phase of your life. But instead of recklessly pushing ahead on your journey, take a few deep breaths, assimilate what has already happened, and reevaluate your plans for what comes next. You may be more inclined to seek out some summertime festivities once physical Mars enters your 5th House of Love and Play on **July 3**, where he remains until **August 23**. But all is not fun and games, as indicated by the serious Capricorn Full Moon—also on **July 3**—that conjuncts extreme Pluto in your 8th House of Transformation. Additionally, trickster Mercury's retrograde phase on **July 14–August 8** occurs in your 3rd House of Immediate Environment, delaying further progress and requiring you to reassess your priorities. Use this time to improve your strategy for following through on the transitions already under way.

Your renewed sense of faith is a reflection of the positive effects of Jupiter, now firmly entrenched

GEMINI 2012

in your sign until next summer. But your positive thinking alone isn't enough to overcome powerful forces that pull you away from your goals when Jupiter forms a frustrating quincunx with domineering Pluto on **July 18**. Although the cautious Cancer New Moon on **July 19** restrains impulsive tendencies, your nerves are on edge and a feeling that anything can happen is in the air. Thankfully an exciting Jupiter-Uranus sextile on **July 22**, followed by a series of supportive aspects indicates smoother sailing through the end of the month as long as you can balance your need for immediate results with the wisdom of long-term planning.

KEEP IN MIND THIS MONTH

You may feel a great sense of urgency to push issues to the next level, but forcing change is not the smartest move now. You have more time than you think.

JULY ♊

KEY DATES

★ JULY 3–4
balancing act

You're ready to risk your comfort by confronting a deep emotional issue on **July 3**, when the ambitious Capricorn Full Moon illuminates your 8th House of Intimacy. Unfortunately, affectionate Venus is more irritating than soothing as she forms an uneasy quincunx with penetrating Pluto. But the current intensity is tempered by the entry of Mars into graceful Libra and your 5th House of Self-Expression. Honest communication should bring positive results as talkative Mercury aspects surprising Uranus and amicable Venus on **July 4**.

★ JULY 8–9
who's on first?

Curious Mercury's skillful quintile to strategic Saturn on **July 8** encourages you to ask smart questions, but a confusing Mars-Neptune quincunx distorts the truth and makes it nearly impossible for you to get your bearings.

Your loss of certainty is further exacerbated by the Sun's anxious aspect to nebulous Neptune on the **9th**. Specific answers may not be forthcoming, but your imagination can fuel a creative process that doesn't need facts.

SUPER NOVA DAYS

★ **JULY 14–17**
no free lunch
You can sweet-talk your way through a sticky situation on **July 14**, when your key planet, Mercury, turns retrograde as it forms a sexy sextile with enchanting Venus. But the Sun's resistant square to constrictive Saturn the next day won't let you sidestep your responsibilities to have a good time or avoid future consequences of your current actions. Impulsive Mars, in your playful 5th House, amplifies your confidence and your energy as he harmoniously trines indulgent Jupiter on **July 17**. Nevertheless, think before you act; an unforgiving Mars-Pluto square on the same day can extract a severe price if you aimlessly pursue a passing pleasure.

JULY ♊

★ JULY 18–22
larger than life

Everything seems bigger and more important on **July 18–22** when inflationary Jupiter aspects Pluto, Saturn, and Uranus, blowing problems out of proportion and presenting solutions that seem better than they actually are. But no single answer appears to resolve a current relationship dilemma. However, anxiety and frustration can catalyze a sudden energetic shift as Mars opposes Uranus on **July 18**. Meanwhile, the nurturing Cancer New Moon on **July 19** in your 2nd House of Self-Worth reminds you that respecting others is easier if you value your own feelings, too.

★ JULY 31
carpe diem

The Sun's trine to impulsive Uranus spurs you to seize the moment, while a stabilizing Venus-Saturn trine allows you to patiently wait for gratification. Fortunately, a quintile between clever Mercury and action-hero Mars shows you a sensible balance between these two extreme approaches to success.

AUGUST

AUGUST

FLYING BY THE SEAT OF YOUR PANTS

This month is full of change and is bound to bring a few surprises along the way. The action starts immediately as the quirky Aquarius Full Moon on **August 1** falls in your 9th House of Adventure, tempting you to dream about the future rather than take care of business in the present moment. But messenger Mercury is still retrograde in your 3rd House of Communication, so it's tough to make progress if you're dealing with delays caused by misunderstandings, incorrect assumptions, or lack of preparation. Fortunately, your efforts should begin to pay off soon after Mercury turns direct on **August 8**, while gracious Venus's entry into nurturing Cancer on **August 7** encourages you to consider other people's feelings before speaking your mind.

Your frustration builds through **August 15**, when hot Mars joins cold Saturn in your 5th House of Romance and Self-Expression, confronting you with unavoidable consequences of recent behavior. Issues about love and money could become more troublesome, yet the dramatic Leo New Moon on

GEMINI 2012

August 17 is a turning point that empowers you to take direct action to resolve recent difficulties. The Sun's entry into efficient Virgo on **August 22** helps you to focus on your intentions. Set specific goals, for little will stand in your way once Mars enters passionate Scorpio and your 6th House of Work on **August 23**. A second Full Moon this month on **August 31** shines in your 10th House of Career in psychic Pisces, strengthening your intuition about the outcome of an important professional decision. Analytical Mercury sharpens your perceptions and fine-tunes your logic as it slips into precise Virgo, also on the **31st**.

KEEP IN MIND THIS MONTH

Although you can see that you're making progress again, you still must handle day-to-day situations as they arise before you think about what comes next.

AUGUST

KEY DATES

★ AUGUST 1–4
spellbound

You catch glimpses of what's around the next bend when the brilliant Aquarius Full Moon on **August 1** illuminates your 9th House of Future Vision. But your optimism may be blinded by the zealous Jupiter-Moon trine that encourages you to expect too much. On **August 2**, the outgoing Leo Sun aspects excessive Jupiter and bewitching Venus, further enticing you with a variety of potentially pleasurable distractions. You could waste time and energy as dreamy Neptune's influence on **August 3–4** has you chasing elusive satisfaction. Show some self-restraint before you suffer the consequences of overindulgence.

★ AUGUST 8–9
it's getting better all the time

You've struggled to keep your life in order since **July 14**, when your key planet, Mercury, turned retrograde. Fortunately, it becomes easier for you to maintain the hectic pace when expressive Mercury turns direct in generous Leo on **August 8**. Others may notice a positive change in your attitude, too, with your words reflecting a new sense of optimism. But don't fool yourself about love or money, because attractive Venus in your 2nd House of Self-Worth trines imaginative Neptune on **August 9**. Visualize the best possible outcome by letting your dreams be your guide, but anchor your logic to reality.

SUPER NOVA DAYS

★ **AUGUST 14–17**
shadow dancing
You can exhaust yourself trying to avoid a difficult lesson about love now—or you can stop rationalizing and delve deeply into your emotions. The Leo Sun's anxious sesquisquares to potent Pluto and shaky Uranus on **August 14–15** put you on notice that there is no stable place to stand as shifting circumstances test your resolve. Additionally, needy Venus in emotional Cancer opposes Pluto and squares Uranus on **August 15–16**,

revealing a darker side of love if you succumb to possessiveness or jealousy. And an inarguable Mars-Saturn conjunction on **August 15** is a reality check that requires you to face current issues head-on. Ultimately, the Leo New Moon on **August 17** rewards your willingness to enter the unknown darkness by shining light on a previously unseen path to success.

★ **AUGUST 24–26**
lost in the hall of mirrors
It's tough to know what's real when the Sun and Venus both form disquieting aspects with surreal Neptune on **August 24**. Disappointment can follow if you allow yourself to be distracted by fantasies of sensual enjoyment rather than utilizing your imagination for more creative purposes. Luckily, a Mars-Neptune trine on **August 26** inspires you to apply your passion to spiritual pursuits instead of transient pleasures.

SEPTEMBER

SEPTEMBER

STORMS OF CHANGE

The second of two long-lasting squares this year between revolutionary Uranus and evolutionary Pluto is exact on **September 19**—although you'll feel its impact for much longer—reactivating issues about your long-term goals that surfaced around **June 24** when this potent pair first aligned. Even if you acknowledge that the direction of your life needs remapping, you might not yet realize the magnitude of the changes that are coming your way over the next few years. Fortunately, compelling Pluto receives positive aspects from assertive Mars, communicator Mercury, and maverick Chiron on **September 3–6**, empowering you to make constructive decisions about family matters and work. Your choices may not be what others expect, but it's more important to maintain your integrity than it is to please everyone else. In fact, several annoying quincunxes that occur this month can place satisfaction just out of your reach. Focus on doing the right thing rather than trying to take the easy way out.

The exacting Virgo New Moon on **September 15** invites you to plant a seed of intention in your 4th

GEMINI 2012

House of Foundations. Don't force resolution to a domestic problem now, because insistent Mars quincunxes exaggerated Jupiter on **September 16**, tempting you to overextend yourself. Fortunately, the stress can feed your creativity, especially when Mercury enters aesthetic Libra and your 5th House of Self-Expression, also on the **16th**, and forms hard aspects with the Uranus-Pluto square on the **20th**. The Autumn Equinox on **September 22** is marked by the Sun's shift into Libra and your 5th House, adding spontaneity to your artistry. Nevertheless, you may feel the tension ratchet up even more when the Aries Full Moon on **September 29** conjuncts jumpy Uranus and squares obsessive Pluto.

KEEP IN MIND THIS MONTH

It's necessary to think on two levels now. Take care of the most pressing issues while also considering the impact your current actions will have on your future.

SEPTEMBER ♊

KEY DATES

★ SEPTEMBER 3-5
all by yourself

You may feel lost and alone on **September 3** when lovable Venus squares judgmental Saturn. Don't wallow in disappointment because a motivating Mars-Pluto sextile empowers you to do something about your current situation. Thankfully, you can find clarity, because astute Mercury trines incisive Pluto on **September 4** and sextiles straightforward Mars on **September 5**. But your friends might not support your sensible initiative the way you expect when Mars and Mercury make unsettling quincunxes to wayward Uranus in your 11th House of Social Networking on **September 4**.

★ SEPTEMBER 7-8
too much of a good thing can hurt

The Sun squares Jupiter on the **7th**, infusing your life with joyful optimism, but also pulling you in two directions. Jupiter in multitasking Gemini tempts you to say yes to every opportunity, but the selective Virgo Sun affirms that you can't do it all. Rational Mercury also squares Jupiter on the **8th**, increasing the contrast between blind optimism and informed realism. Exercise self-control or you'll exhaust yourself before you reach your goal.

★ **SEPTEMBER 12–16**
rock and roll star
It's not easy to keep your desires in check when sensual Venus quincunxes passionate Pluto on the **12th**, and you may want to try something new when Venus trines experimental Uranus on the **13th**. Luckily, a practical Virgo New Moon on the **15th** can bring you back to earth, but it might not be enough to snap you out of your mistaken belief that you can do anything you want. Be especially cautious on the **16th**, when a Mars-Jupiter quincunx gives you a false sense of invincibility.

★ **SEPTEMBER 20**
give peace a chance
The more you talk, the more complicated everything becomes as verbose Mercury in

SEPTEMBER ♊

your expressive 5th House opposes shocking Uranus and squares mighty Pluto. Instead of trying to win the debate, stop arguing and allow the sweet Venus-Jupiter sextile to show you how to enjoy yourself in the present moment.

SUPER NOVA DAYS

★ **SEPTEMBER 25-29**
rocky road

You may be tempted to gamble with your stability in a risky scheme to regain more control of your life. On **September 25-26** uncomfortable aspects from Mars and Venus to the lingering Uranus-Pluto square can reignite a disagreement that you thought was resolved. The pressure to change dysfunctional relationship dynamics continues to mount through **September 29** when the Libra Sun in your 5th House of Romance and the impulsive Aries Full Moon in your 11th House of Dreams and Wishes both stress volcanic Uranus and Pluto.

OCTOBER

OCTOBER ♊

CHANGE OF PACE

Take time out from all the pressures for change this month and consider which opportunities merit further exploration. When expansive Jupiter turns retrograde in your sign on **October 4**, it's wise to withdraw from the chaos and noise of your everyday life so you can listen to your own inner voice instead of being distracted by everyone else's opinions. This soulful deepening of your life is punctuated by rational Mercury on **October 5** when it joins somber Saturn as they both enter emotional Scorpio and your 6th House of Self-Improvement. You are less interested now in changing the world than in correcting those things that aren't working optimally in your daily routine. On **October 10**, however, traditional Saturn forms a long-lasting trine with inspirational Neptune in your 10th House of Career—the first in a series of three that culminates on **July 19, 2013**—motivating you to work methodically toward manifesting your professional dreams.

A bit of levity arrives to lighten the mood when the creative Libra New Moon on **October 15** spotlights your 5th House of Fun and Games. A friend or partner may surprise you with unexpected behavior since assertive Mars in your 7th House of Relationships trines unpredictable Uranus. Although you may gain more freedom, an imbalanced sesquisquare between optimistic Jupiter and pessimistic Saturn reveals uncertainty about how to reach your goals. Your resolve intensifies when the Sun enters inflexible Scorpio on **October 22**, yet the Taurus Full Moon in your 12th House of Escapism on **October 29** can be confusing as you seek comfort from your dreams and fantasies.

KEEP IN MIND THIS MONTH

Your newfound vision of the future eases your stress and gives you time to reconsider where you want your life to go.

OCTOBER ♊

KEY DATES

★ OCTOBER 3–7
the uncertainty principle

You feel disoriented when lovely Venus opposes foggy Neptune in your 10th House of Status on **October 3** and journeying Jupiter turns retrograde on **October 4**, making it difficult to find direction in your life. Cerebral Mercury runs into solemn Saturn on **October 5**, adding weight to your thoughts. Luckily, a Mercury-Neptune trine encourages dreaming and gives you hope. Although you are drawn to others when ardent Mars enters outgoing Sagittarius and your 7th House of Companions on **October 6**, the misleading Mars-Neptune square on **October 7** reminds you that success will remain elusive as long as you're chasing an unrealizable dream.

SUPER NOVA DAYS

★ OCTOBER 9–10
positive vibrations

You are on top of your game on **October 9**, when the Sun in your 5th House of Fun forms a lovely trine to lucky Jupiter. Romantic Venus trines transformational Pluto in your 8th House of Intimacy to deepen your joy. Messenger Mercury's cooperative sextile to Pluto on the **10th** gives you the words to describe your intense feelings. Additionally, persistent Saturn connects with otherworldly Neptune to open a direct channel between the real world and your imagination. You skillfully blend material and spiritual pursuits now as you look to your future.

★ OCTOBER 15–16
over your limit

You can successfully break out of a rut when impetuous Mars trines electric Uranus just prior to the diplomatic Libra New Moon on **October 15**. You're capable of outsmarting your co-workers when persuasive Mercury sextiles disarming Venus on **October 16**. Unfortunately, stressful aspects to flamboyant Jupiter on both days embolden you to overestimate your resources. Unless you know your limitations and respect other people's boundaries, you could lose all that you stand to gain.

OCTOBER

★ **OCTOBER 25**
reality check
Even if you believe that you're on track with your progress, the Sun's conjunction with stern Saturn in your 6th House of Employment today indicates a temporary setback as you face the facts you tried to avoid. Instead of attempting to work around the issues, learn the lessons they are trying to teach you before moving on.

★ **OCTOBER 28-29**
the power of persistence
Your enthusiasm knows no bounds when an enthusiastic Mars-Jupiter opposition activates your 7th House of Relationships on **October 28**. Someone might try to steer you off course by misrepresenting the truth as Mercury squares delusional Neptune on the **29th**. However, the stubborn Taurus Full Moon trines unyielding Pluto, so you won't be led astray if you make up your mind and stick to it.

NOVEMBER

NOVEMBER

HURRY UP AND WAIT

This is a month of delays that you can use to your advantage once you accept that things will take longer than you've planned. You may need to put relationship issues on the front burner when Mercury starts backtracking in your 7th House of Partners on **November 6**. However, your daily routine is affected, too, for mental Mercury reenters your 6th House of Work on **November 14**, remaining there through **December 10**. Although the heavenly messenger turns direct on **November 26**, its sluggish movement through the end of the month means that you could actually lose ground as you review recent mistakes, reconsider your assumptions, redo your calendar, and reinvent your strategy for success. You may grow frustrated with your lack of momentum and attempt to speed things up, but to no avail. Don't think that you have failed if something slips through the cracks. Instead, make a commitment to be patient and dig deeper than ever before to uncover the information that will allow you to improve the quality of your daily life.

GEMINI 2012

Two eclipses—a Solar Eclipse on **November 13** and a Lunar Eclipse on **November 28**—overwhelm you with an abundance of nervous tension. You feel as if you're standing on a precipice and must take exactly the right step to prevent misfortune. The transformational Scorpio New Moon Eclipse on the **13th** is a great time to initiate improvements in your diet and exercise regimen, because it activates your 6th House of Health and Habits. The Gemini Full Moon Eclipse on the **28th** joins propitious Jupiter in your 12th House of Destiny, supporting renewed faith that your hard work will soon be rewarded.

KEEP IN MIND THIS MONTH

If you're just spinning your wheels and getting nowhere fast, back up, catch your breath, reassess your approach, and try again.

NOVEMBER ♊

KEY DATES

★ NOVEMBER 1–3
easy does it

If you feel blocked by a co-worker on **November 1** when contentious Mars stressfully semisquares bossy Saturn, an angry response isn't your smartest move. Instead, use the unconventional Venus-Uranus opposition to seek a more innovative solution. Surprise others with your uncharacteristic intensity when charismatic Venus squares powerhouse Pluto on **November 3**. But don't go overboard and turn a good thing into a major drama.

★ NOVEMBER 9–11
sweet escape

Flirty Venus in your 5th House of Love and Play forms a delicious trine with opulent Jupiter on **November 9**, replacing problems with pleasure. A fantasy-prone Venus-Neptune alignment further inspires you to believe in your dreams. But a disappointing semisquare between social Mercury and Venus on **November 11** can sour the stew and take the fun out of a delightful conversation if you hold on to unrealistic expectations.

SUPER NOVA DAYS

★ NOVEMBER 13-17
out of your element
Entering strange territory may not feel easy on the **13th** when the enigmatic Scorpio New Moon Eclipse forces you to leave language behind and jump into an emotional abyss. You may feel cross from Mercury's square to Neptune on the **13th** or by Mercury's entry into Scorpio on the **14th**. Saturn aligns with Chiron on the **16th**, offering healing compassion. Although energetic Mars enters persistent Capricorn and your 8th House of Regeneration the same day to push you along on your path, Mars's sextile to Neptune on the **17th** favors a spiritual awakening that can catalyze a deep restoration of your well-being.

★ NOVEMBER 22-24
lost and found
You struggle to get an accurate sense of what's happening with your career when

NOVEMBER

hazy Neptune in your 10th House of Public Life squares the Sun and trines Venus on **November 22**. You may be so freaked out with your inability to decide upon a course of action that a volatile Mars-Uranus square on the **23rd** could provoke radical action that you haven't thought out very well. Luckily, a skillful Mars-Saturn sextile the next day helps you to quickly bring some stability back into your life.

★ NOVEMBER 26–29
don't look back

Mercury's direct turn on **November 26**, coupled with the fidgety Gemini Full Moon Eclipse on **November 28**, sets the stage for your next wave of progress. But advancement does not come easily, because the austere Venus-Saturn conjunction on the **26th** forces you to narrow your objectives. Although an aggressive Mars-Pluto conjunction on the **27th** emboldens you to fight for your beliefs, gentler aspects on **November 28–29** allow you to move on without holding on to any unnecessary negativity.

DECEMBER

DECEMBER   ♊

OVER THE RAINBOW

Now that your key planet, Mercury, is moving direct again, you should begin to notice progress on several fronts. But with jolly Jupiter visiting your sign this year, you can't help but be happily distracted by the holiday hustle and bustle. On **December 2**, the illuminating Sun in uplifting Sagittarius opposes Jupiter from your 7th House of Others, shining a positive light on anyone who brings you opportunities for growth and the potential for adventurous experiences. As long as you don't go overboard blindly seeking a good time, joyful Jupiter is your good-luck charm now. Messenger Mercury becomes even chattier when it enters gregarious Sagittarius and your 7th House on **December 10** and could deliver good news when it opposes Jupiter on **December 17**. Entertaining Venus follows Mercury to join the lively party in your 7th House on **December 15**, and then takes the fun to the next level when she opposes outrageous Jupiter on **December 22**.

The upbeat Sagittarius New Moon on **December 13** confirms this new cycle of optimism, tempting you to agree with your friends and co-workers without doing any critical thinking of your own. Meanwhile, serious Saturn slowly moves toward a supportive sextile with formidable Pluto that's exact on **December 26**. This long-lasting aspect gives you the power to thrive during big changes. But as good as all this sounds, Jupiter forms an unsatisfying quincunx with Pluto on **December 20** and with Saturn on the **22nd**, prompting you to question whether success is even worth the effort. A wave of fear washes in with the worried Cancer Full Moon in your 2nd House of Self-Worth on **December 28**. This lunation opposes relentless Pluto and can remind you of the inevitability of change, which, thankfully, you can handle better than most.

KEEP IN MIND THIS MONTH

It's easy for you to scatter your energy and have nothing to show for your efforts. Enjoying yourself is important, but keep some resources in reserve.

DECEMBER

KEY DATES

★ **DECEMBER 1–2**
act as if . . .
You grow anxious during the nervous Mercury-Uranus aspect on **December 1**, but you should be able to conceal your worries. Animated Mars and alluring Venus both form uncomfortable quincunxes with loud Jupiter, motivating you to overcompensate for any uncertainty by boldly describing your needs and stating how you will fulfill them. But you don't need to prove to anyone else what you can do. If you believe in yourself, then others will jump on the bandwagon as the Sun opposes Jupiter in your 1st House of Self on **December 2**.

★ **DECEMBER 10–14**
into the great wide open
Your fantasies can stretch the bounds of your creativity when inquisitive Mercury enters inspirational Sagittarius on **December 10** and squares irrational Neptune on **December 11**. Luckily, an innovative quintile between

physical Mars and hardworking Saturn on the **12th** restores balance by giving you tools to manifest your vision, however unrealistic it may seem. The extroverted Sagittarius New Moon on the **13th** falls in your 7th House of Partnerships, prompting you to involve someone else in your new project. Mercury's unrestrained trine to progressive Uranus on **December 14** frees your mind, empowering you to take an unproven idea from concept to fulfillment fast enough to make heads spin.

★ **DECEMBER 19–22**
variety is the spice of life
You want to indulge yourself in a plethora of exciting new activities when insatiable Venus trines restless Uranus on **December 19**. Venus's opposition to extravagant Jupiter on **December 22** continues to offer you more pleasurable options. But the Sun's entry into conservative Capricorn on **December 21** marks the Winter Solstice, a time to rest before cranking up the engines of ambition once more. Unfortunately, complex aspects from uninhibited Jupiter in your 1st House of

DECEMBER

Personality to Pluto and Saturn on **December 20–22** make it hard to know whether you should push harder or back off. Success depends on finding a middle path that allows steady progress.

SUPER NOVA DAYS
★ **DECEMBER 28–31**
out with a bang!

You say good-bye to a year full of change with an opportunistic sextile from fiery Mars in your 9th House of Future Vision to wild and crazy Uranus in your 11th House of Friends on **December 31**—and this may be the perfect send-off. Still, the days leading up to New Year's Eve are fraught with emotional traps as the sentimental Cancer Full Moon on **December 28** floods you with memories that may be difficult to express. Keep the communication channels open; the Sun conjuncts intense Pluto in your 8th House of Intimacy on **December 30**, pushing suppressed feelings to the surface. Cleaning up old emotional business permits you to move forward with a clear conscience.

APPENDIXES

★

2012 MONTH-AT-A-GLANCE ASTROCALENDAR

★

FAMOUS GEMINIS

★

GEMINI IN LOVE

JANUARY 2012

SUNDAY 1 ★ The feedback you receive now could help you in the future

---

MONDAY 2
TUESDAY 3
WEDNESDAY 4
THURSDAY 5
FRIDAY 6
SATURDAY 7 ★ **SUPER NOVA DAYS** Honor your own feelings

SUNDAY 8
MONDAY 9 ★ ○
TUESDAY 10
WEDNESDAY 11
THURSDAY 12 ★ Roll up your sleeves and get to work

FRIDAY 13 ★
SATURDAY 14
SUNDAY 15
MONDAY 16
TUESDAY 17
WEDNESDAY 18
THURSDAY 19
FRIDAY 20
SATURDAY 21 ★ Great adventures are on your mind

SUNDAY 22 ★
MONDAY 23 ★ ●
TUESDAY 24
WEDNESDAY 25
THURSDAY 26
FRIDAY 27 ★ A setback reveals a flaw in your plan

SATURDAY 28 ★
SUNDAY 29
MONDAY 30
TUESDAY 31

★ designates key date

FEBRUARY 2012

WEDNESDAY 1 ★ Don't start an unnecessary fight

THURSDAY 2

FRIDAY 3

SATURDAY 4

SUNDAY 5

MONDAY 6

TUESDAY 7 ★ ○ **SUPER NOVA DAYS** Do things differently

WEDNESDAY 8 ★

THURSDAY 9 ★

FRIDAY 10 ★

SATURDAY 11

SUNDAY 12

MONDAY 13

TUESDAY 14 ★ A struggle for control could get out of hand

WEDNESDAY 15 ★

THURSDAY 16 ★

FRIDAY 17 ★

SATURDAY 18 ★

SUNDAY 19

MONDAY 20

TUESDAY 21 ★ ● Apologize, if necessary, and then move on

WEDNESDAY 22 ★

THURSDAY 23 ★

FRIDAY 24

SATURDAY 25

SUNDAY 26

MONDAY 27

TUESDAY 28 ★ You are at the top of your game

WEDNESDAY 29

MARCH 2012

THURSDAY 1 ★ Pick your battles wisely

FRIDAY 2 ★
SATURDAY 3 ★
SUNDAY 4
MONDAY 5 ★ Turn your brainstorm into reality

TUESDAY 6
WEDNESDAY 7
THURSDAY 8 ○
FRIDAY 9
SATURDAY 10
SUNDAY 11
MONDAY 12 ★ **SUPER NOVA DAYS** You are lucky in love or money

---

TUESDAY 13 ★
WEDNESDAY 14 ★
THURSDAY 15
FRIDAY 16
SATURDAY 17
SUNDAY 18
MONDAY 19
TUESDAY 20
WEDNESDAY 21
THURSDAY 22 ●
FRIDAY 23
SATURDAY 24
SUNDAY 25
MONDAY 26 ★ Modify your long-term goals

TUESDAY 27 ★
WEDNESDAY 28 ★
THURSDAY 29 ★
FRIDAY 30
SATURDAY 31

APRIL 2012

SUNDAY 1

MONDAY 2

TUESDAY 3

WEDNESDAY 4 ★ Be completely honest with all involved

THURSDAY 5 ★

FRIDAY 6 ★ ○

SATURDAY 7 ★

SUNDAY 8

MONDAY 9

TUESDAY 10

WEDNESDAY 11

THURSDAY 12 ★ Hard work is your current key to success

FRIDAY 13 ★

SATURDAY 14 ★

SUNDAY 15 ★

MONDAY 16 ★

TUESDAY 17

WEDNESDAY 18

THURSDAY 19

FRIDAY 20 ★ **SUPER NOVA DAYS** Defend your innovative ideas

SATURDAY 21 ★ ●

SUNDAY 22 ★

MONDAY 23 ★

TUESDAY 24

WEDNESDAY 25 ★ Fear is no match for the truth

THURSDAY 26

FRIDAY 27

SATURDAY 28

SUNDAY 29 ★ An unstoppable wave of change washes through your life

MONDAY 30

MAY 2012

TUESDAY 1	
WEDNESDAY 2	
THURSDAY 3	
FRIDAY 4	
SATURDAY 5 ★	○ Take a leap of faith

SUNDAY 6 ★	
MONDAY 7 ★	
TUESDAY 8	
WEDNESDAY 9	
THURSDAY 10	
FRIDAY 11	
SATURDAY 12	
SUNDAY 13 ★	Use your time wisely by preparing for what's ahead

MONDAY 14 ★	
TUESDAY 15 ★	
WEDNESDAY 16 ★	
THURSDAY 17	
FRIDAY 18	
SATURDAY 19	
SUNDAY 20 ★	● **SUPER NOVA DAYS** Tap into a creative flow

MONDAY 21 ★	
TUESDAY 22 ★	
WEDNESDAY 23	
THURSDAY 24	
FRIDAY 25	
SATURDAY 26	
SUNDAY 27 ★	Share your radical ideas with friends

MONDAY 28 ★	
TUESDAY 29 ★	
WEDNESDAY 30 ★	
THURSDAY 31	

JUNE 2012

FRIDAY 1

SATURDAY 2

SUNDAY 3 ★ Settle down and take yourself seriously

MONDAY 4 ★ ○

TUESDAY 5 ★

WEDNESDAY 6

THURSDAY 7

FRIDAY 8

SATURDAY 9

SUNDAY 10

MONDAY 11 ★ Self-restraint is advised now

TUESDAY 12 ★

WEDNESDAY 13 ★

THURSDAY 14

FRIDAY 15

SATURDAY 16

SUNDAY 17

MONDAY 18

TUESDAY 19 ★ ● Confront the shortcomings of your escape plan

WEDNESDAY 20 ★

THURSDAY 21 ★

FRIDAY 22

SATURDAY 23

SUNDAY 24

MONDAY 25

TUESDAY 26

WEDNESDAY 27 ★ **SUPER NOVA DAYS** Changes are coming fast and furious

THURSDAY 28 ★

FRIDAY 29 ★

SATURDAY 30

JULY 2012

SUNDAY 1	
MONDAY 2	
TUESDAY 3 ★	○ Honest communication should bring positive results

WEDNESDAY 4 ★	
THURSDAY 5	
FRIDAY 6	
SATURDAY 7	
SUNDAY 8 ★	Imagination can fuel your creative process

MONDAY 9 ★	
TUESDAY 10	
WEDNESDAY 11	
THURSDAY 12	
FRIDAY 13	
SATURDAY 14 ★	**SUPER NOVA DAYS** Think before you act

SUNDAY 15 ★	
MONDAY 16 ★	
TUESDAY 17 ★	
WEDNESDAY 18 ★	Everything seems bigger and more important than it is

THURSDAY 19 ★ ●	
FRIDAY 20 ★	
SATURDAY 21 ★	
SUNDAY 22 ★	
MONDAY 23	
TUESDAY 24	
WEDNESDAY 25	
THURSDAY 26	
FRIDAY 27	
SATURDAY 28	
SUNDAY 29	
MONDAY 30	
TUESDAY 31 ★	Moderate your approach to success

AUGUST 2012

WEDNESDAY 1 ★ ○ You could waste time and energy chasing your dreams

THURSDAY 2 ★
FRIDAY 3 ★
SATURDAY 4 ★
SUNDAY 5
MONDAY 6
TUESDAY 7
WEDNESDAY 8 ★ Don't fool yourself about love or money

THURSDAY 9 ★
FRIDAY 10
SATURDAY 11
SUNDAY 12
MONDAY 13
TUESDAY 14 ★ SUPER NOVA DAYS Face current issues head-on

WEDNESDAY 15 ★
THURSDAY 16 ★
FRIDAY 17 ★ ●
SATURDAY 18
SUNDAY 19
MONDAY 20
TUESDAY 21
WEDNESDAY 22
THURSDAY 23
FRIDAY 24 ★ Apply your passion to spiritual pursuits

SATURDAY 25 ★
SUNDAY 26 ★
MONDAY 27
TUESDAY 28
WEDNESDAY 29
THURSDAY 30
FRIDAY 31 ○

SEPTEMBER 2012

SATURDAY 1	
SUNDAY 2	
MONDAY 3 ★	Don't wallow in disappointment
TUESDAY 4 ★	
WEDNESDAY 5 ★	
THURSDAY 6	
FRIDAY 7 ★	Be wise and exercise self-control
SATURDAY 8 ★	
SUNDAY 9	
MONDAY 10	
TUESDAY 11	
WEDNESDAY 12 ★	It's not easy to keep your desires in check
THURSDAY 13 ★	
FRIDAY 14 ★	
SATURDAY 15 ★ ●	
SUNDAY 16 ★	
MONDAY 17	
TUESDAY 18	
WEDNESDAY 19	
THURSDAY 20 ★	Enjoy yourself in the present moment
FRIDAY 21	
SATURDAY 22	
SUNDAY 23	
MONDAY 24	
TUESDAY 25 ★	**SUPER NOVA DAYS** The pressure to change continues to build
WEDNESDAY 26 ★	
THURSDAY 27 ★	
FRIDAY 28 ★	
SATURDAY 29 ★ ○	
SUNDAY 30	

OCTOBER 2012

MONDAY 1	
TUESDAY 2	
WEDNESDAY 3 ★	It's difficult to find direction in your life
THURSDAY 4 ★	
FRIDAY 5 ★	
SATURDAY 6 ★	
SUNDAY 7 ★	
MONDAY 8	
TUESDAY 9 ★	**SUPER NOVA DAYS** Blend material and spiritual pursuits
WEDNESDAY 10 ★	
THURSDAY 11	
FRIDAY 12	
SATURDAY 13	
SUNDAY 14	
MONDAY 15 ★ ●	Know your limitations
TUESDAY 16 ★	
WEDNESDAY 17 ★	
THURSDAY 18	
FRIDAY 19	
SATURDAY 20	
SUNDAY 21	
MONDAY 22	
TUESDAY 23	
WEDNESDAY 24	
THURSDAY 25 ★	Face the facts
FRIDAY 26	
SATURDAY 27	
SUNDAY 28 ★	Make up your mind and stick to it
MONDAY 29 ★ ○	
TUESDAY 30	
WEDNESDAY 31	

NOVEMBER 2012

THURSDAY 1 ★ Seek innovative solutions

FRIDAY 2 ★
SATURDAY 3 ★
SUNDAY 4
MONDAY 5
TUESDAY 6
WEDNESDAY 7
THURSDAY 8

FRIDAY 9 ★ Believe in your dreams

SATURDAY 10 ★
SUNDAY 11 ★
MONDAY 12
TUESDAY 13 ★ ● **SUPER NOVA DAYS** Enter unfamiliar territory

WEDNESDAY 14 ★
THURSDAY 15 ★
FRIDAY 16 ★
SATURDAY 17 ★
SUNDAY 18
MONDAY 19
TUESDAY 20
WEDNESDAY 21

THURSDAY 22 ★ Your uncertainty could provoke radical action

FRIDAY 23 ★
SATURDAY 24 ★
SUNDAY 25

MONDAY 26 ★ Narrow your objectives

TUESDAY 27 ★
WEDNESDAY 28 ★ ○
THURSDAY 29 ★
FRIDAY 30

DECEMBER 2012

SATURDAY 1 ★ Believe in yourself

SUNDAY 2 ★

MONDAY 3

TUESDAY 4

WEDNESDAY 5

THURSDAY 6

FRIDAY 7

SATURDAY 8

SUNDAY 9

MONDAY 10 ★ Your fantasies can stretch the bounds of your creativity

---

TUESDAY 11 ★

WEDNESDAY 12 ★

THURSDAY 13 ★ ●

FRIDAY 14 ★

SATURDAY 15

SUNDAY 16

MONDAY 17

TUESDAY 18

WEDNESDAY 19 ★ Success depends on finding a middle path

THURSDAY 20 ★

FRIDAY 21 ★

SATURDAY 22 ★

SUNDAY 23

MONDAY 24

TUESDAY 25

WEDNESDAY 26

THURSDAY 27

FRIDAY 28 ★ ○ **SUPER NOVA DAYS** Keep the communication channels open

---

SATURDAY 29 ★

SUNDAY 30 ★

MONDAY 31 ★

FAMOUS GEMINIS

Mr. T	★	5/21/1952
Notorious B.I.G.	★	5/21/1972
Al Franken	★	5/21/1951
Sir Arthur Conan Doyle	★	5/22/1859
Sir Laurence Olivier	★	5/22/1907
Joan Collins	★	5/23/1933
Bob Dylan	★	5/24/1941
Ralph Waldo Emerson	★	5/25/1803
Lauryn Hill	★	5/25/1975
John Wayne	★	5/26/1907
Stevie Nicks	★	5/26/1948
Pam Grier	★	5/26/1949
Lenny Kravitz	★	5/26/1964
Dashiell Hammett	★	5/27/1894
Vincent Price	★	5/27/1911
Rudolph Giuliani	★	5/28/1944
Kylie Minogue	★	5/28/1968
Patrick Henry	★	5/29/1736
Bob Hope	★	5/29/1903
John F. Kennedy	★	5/29/1917
Melissa Etheridge	★	5/29/1961
Wynonna Judd	★	5/30/1964
Walt Whitman	★	5/31/1819
Clint Eastwood	★	5/31/1930
Brooke Shields	★	5/31/1965
Colin Farrell	★	5/31/1976
Marilyn Monroe	★	6/1/1926
Morgan Freeman	★	6/1/1937
Alanis Morissette	★	6/1/1974
Josephine Baker	★	6/3/1906
Tony Curtis	★	6/3/1925
Allen Ginsberg	★	6/3/1926
Curtis Mayfield	★	6/3/1942
Dr. Ruth Westheimer	★	6/4/1928
Angelina Jolie	★	6/4/1975
Dean Martin	★	6/7/1917
Allen Iverson	★	6/7/1975

FAMOUS GEMINIS

Anna Kournikova	★	6/7/1981
Prince	★	6/7/1958
Frank Lloyd Wright	★	6/8/1867
Barbara Bush	★	6/8/1925
Nancy Sinatra	★	6/8/1940
Cole Porter	★	6/9/1891
Les Paul	★	6/9/1915
Johnny Depp	★	6/9/1963
Michael J. Fox	★	6/9/1961
Judy Garland	★	6/10/1922
Maurice Sendak	★	6/10/1928
Jacques Cousteau	★	6/11/1910
Joe Montana	★	6/11/1956
George H. W. Bush	★	6/12/1924
Anne Frank	★	6/12/1929
William Butler Yeats	★	6/13/1865
Mary-Kate and Ashley Olsen	★	6/13/1986
Harriet Beecher Stowe	★	6/14/1811
Donald Trump	★	6/14/1946
Boy George	★	6/14/1961
Helen Hunt	★	6/15/1963
Ice Cube	★	6/15/1969
Joyce Carol Oates	★	6/16/1938
Tupac Shakur	★	6/16/1971
Igor Stravinsky	★	6/17/1882
M. C. Escher	★	6/17/1898
Newt Gingrich	★	6/17/1943
Venus Williams	★	6/17/1980
Roger Ebert	★	6/18/1942
Paul McCartney	★	6/18/1942
Lou Gehrig	★	6/19/1903
Salman Rushdie	★	6/19/1947
Paula Abdul	★	6/19/1962
Lionel Richie	★	6/20/1949
Nicole Kidman	★	6/20/1967

GEMINI IN LOVE

GEMINI & ARIES (MARCH 21–APRIL 19)

Your spontaneity mixes well with action-oriented Aries, making a lighthearted and congenial couple. You both usually choose to experience the brighter side of life. Together you contribute your share of joy to the world around you. Communication is very important to you, and in many ways you actually express your love through ideas and the words used to share them. Your Aries lover, on the other hand, is less inclined to intellectualism and is more tactile and immediate. He or she will need some independence and your comings and goings should provide them with enough freedom so that they don't feel too constrained by the demands of the relationship. Will this one last? It's hard to tell, but one thing is certain. You're going to have to make things feel new and exciting for your Aries to stay interested. If your love planet, Venus, is in Aries, then this won't be a problem. It may take some effort to create long-term stability, but you and your Aries friend can inspire each other to invent new and potent ways to express ideas and to lead the way toward a life that you both can enjoy.

GEMINI IN LOVE

GEMINI & TAURUS (APRIL 20–MAY 20)

Your lighthearted and fast-moving mind finds solid ground to rest upon when you team up with a more practical and levelheaded Taurus. The problem is that you may quickly become bored, unless your Moon is in an earth sign (Taurus, Virgo, or Capricorn) or your Mercury is in Taurus. Regardless of other planetary locations, your fast reflexes and agile constitution are quite different from Taurus's slowly deliberate and determined manner. If you can get past your differences in style, the two of you can really enjoy the company of one another. Your mate puts you at rest and allows you to stop spinning your wheels, which lets you make better use of your creative potential. Your brilliant abilities flourish as you put your ideas into a solid format that can be shared with others and built upon. On the other hand, you are the sales person who can promote the Taurus's fine reputation and solid integrity. Although your flirtatious nature may irritate your lover, he or she will stand by you through thick and thin, as long as you don't overdo it.

GEMINI IN LOVE

GEMINI & GEMINI (MAY 21–JUNE 20)

For the most part, people who share the same sun sign have a tremendous amount in common. However, some of the duo sun-sign combinations share their traits more harmoniously than others do. As an air Gemini whose restless mind is always moving, you tend to clash a bit more with a fellow Gemini than other duos. You are such a mercurial chatterbox that in an intimate relationship with another Twin, you may be so busy conjuring clever responses before the other has finished a sentence that you don't really listen to what your equally talkative partner is saying. Obviously, this can cause problems and may create agitation. If you each have your Moon in a water or earth sign, there's a higher level of compatibility and an easy way beyond this problem. No matter what sign your Moon is in, if you learn to focus on your partner rather than just listening to yourself talk, you can dynamically raise each other to new heights. Remember, this relationship is a mental one, and the sexual attraction here is based on the mutual appreciation of the words you share. Together you can be all talk and no action unless you make a real effort to take care of the practical things in your life.

GEMINI & CANCER (JUNE 21–JULY 22)

You are attracted to movement and change. You love parties, meetings, and social engagements—anything where you get to share ideas and exchange words with like-minded people. Your Cancer lover, on the other hand, is not so driven by a need to interact with others. He or she is more attracted to security and home-centered activities, finding satisfaction from nurturing family and loved ones. Your hard-shelled partner is a tenacious Crab and won't easily let go of the past, while you're ready for whatever the present may bring. It boils down to the fact that your Cancer amour is an emotional water sign and you live in airy mental realms, making for different priorities in your everyday lives. However, if your Venus is in Taurus or Cancer, you'll easily appreciate your partner's stay-at-home attitude. Wherever your other planets are, it's essential for you to learn the value of emotional expression, even if it makes you uncomfortable. If you can slow down and let your feelings catch up with your thoughts, your sensitive Cancer friend will add meaning and richness to your life. Ultimately, the two of you find compatibility only if you can find a balance between your feelings and your thoughts.

GEMINI & LEO (JULY 23–AUGUST 22)

Let's face it: you love to flirt and play. The good news is that your Leo mate loves to be flirted with and adored. The playful Lion is usually ready for a good time, but will separate work and play more than you do. If you can find a way to bring lighthearted fun into your time together, you can be highly compatible. Your habit of looking over the fence for greener pastures will not bode well with the possessive Leo, who needs to be the center of your world, along with plenty of immediate attention and applause. You'll have to beware not to hurt your proud Lion's feelings by flaunting interest elsewhere, or your Leo will retreat. If your Venus is in Leo, this may not be a problem. On the upside, your partner will always communicate through his or her heart with generosity and love. There aren't many things better than being loved by a Leo when they are bestowing their grace upon you. Your keen mental wit is attractive to Leo, but your sarcasm may be too much at times. The long-term possibilities may rest on your willingness to learn the virtues of loving communication.

GEMINI & VIRGO (AUGUST 23–SEPT. 22)

With Virgo, you may have found your mental match. This can be good news or bad news, for your thinking styles are very different from one another. Both of you are ruled by the planet Mercury, which governs the mental aspects of the personality, creating quite an analytical and heady relationship. Whereas you are openly expressive and as curious as any cat, your Virgo partner may see you as a bit scattered within your daily focus—or lack of it. If Mercury or Venus is in Taurus in your chart, however, you'll be more focused and compatibility will be much easier. No matter where your other planets are, Virgo can be impatient with you. Meanwhile, you will probably get annoyed by the nitpicky attitudes of your Virgo mate. His or her personality can be somewhat critical, focusing too much on minute details that you think are irrelevant. Harmonious activities that you can share involve reading and discussing books, writing projects, movies, puzzles, and talking about politics or other intellectual topics. You both appreciate the virtue of intelligence—romantic interplay involves wit and candor.

GEMINI & LIBRA (SEPT. 23–OCT. 22)

This is usually a very good combination, for both you and your Libran love are refined and socially aware. Although you may be a little faster with the clever reply, your partner brings a highly developed sense of grace and style that you can incorporate into your everyday life. Creativity is important to you, and this relationship offers the possibility of working together in the visual arts, writing, or music. You can admire each other's taste in food, clothing, and home decorating, although you tend to have more variety than your color-conscious partner. A shared living space works well and would probably include many beautiful books in an atmosphere of sophistication and harmony. Together, you synchronize your energies into a symphony of beauty, through words and images. Of course, individual relationships are more complex than simple sun signs, and your individual Moon signs can create emotional tensions, depending upon their position. Since you both love to entertain, this relationship offers much to your friends and family. In fact, your ultimate compatibility may depend upon sharing your social life, and in doing so, you can shine together in many ways.

GEMINI & SCORPIO (OCT. 23–NOV. 21)

Have you ever thought about ice-skating on hot lava? You like to glide over the surface without much resistance. On the other hand, your Scorpio lover needs the depth of passion. Unless your Moon is in Scorpio or another water sign, you'd prefer to treat passion intellectually rather than physically. Regardless, it's very important for this relationship to be given time to grow. At first impression, your Scorpio will think that you're superficial and perhaps even shallow. The truth is that without Venus or Mars in a water sign, you may not be able or willing to fulfill your lover's need for intense feelings and focused attention. Scorpio may be attracted to your quick wit and cleverness, which will give you time to show your deeper stuff. At first, you may feel exposed by the deeply intimate approach of your Scorpio partner, but in time, you can find an attractive meeting place in mental and physical attraction. Sexy Scorpio explores new ways to involve you in passionate interplay, and your flirtatiousness responds to the depth of Scorpio's interest with sensual and playful charm and charisma. Even if you can't make it last forever, you can experience the intensity of a great love affair.

GEMINI & SAGITTARIUS (NOV. 22–DEC. 21)

You like movement in your life, in your mind, and in your relationships. Your natural curiosity cannot be squelched. With a Sagittarius, you meet someone who is also interested in activity, but the Archer's arrow tends to aim far—Sagittarians are attracted to long journeys rather than lots of little trips. You are most compatible with your Sagittarius within the context of travel and adventure. He or she will share your restlessness, and together you're on the move. If your individual charts are incompatible in Mars, you may have difficulty finding common ground for your adventures. With Sagittarius, you find it easy to be open-minded, and the Archer's global awareness is exciting to you. Together you could plan a climbing expedition or a biking trip across southern France. The two of you can keep each other well occupied with good humor and intelligent conversation. This relationship is good for you as your Sagittarian lover tends to bring out the optimistic side of your life. Together, you can create a cheerful and bright home life. You two are quite compatible and can have a lasting and satisfying relationship for many years, although it may not ever feel fully stable.

GEMINI & CAPRICORN (DEC. 22–JAN. 19)

You are the quick-change artist known for your restless mind and clever wit. Your Capricorn lover is steady, conservative, and not inclined toward light cocktail-party banter. Gemini's character is very different from the Goat's. Whereas you're playful and childlike, searching for ways to communicate ideas with others, your Goat is serious and hardworking, preferring to focus on tasks and goals. Bridging the gap between these two can be extremely rewarding. Your role in the relationship is to help your Capricorn lighten up the load of daily life with your usual upbeat enthusiasm. Meanwhile, your partner can bring steadfast organization into your life. If Venus or Mars in your chart is compatible with your Capricorn lover's chart, then you'll be more open to creating a strong foundation between the two of you. Quiet Capricorn may need to give plenty of attention to talkative Gemini, learning to appreciate candor as well as a playful approach to communication. It will probably be easier for you to allow for the diverse qualities in each other, but if your Goat can loosen up, it's possible for the two of you to join forces, creating a productive relationship with plenty of room for growth and mutual respect.

GEMINI IN LOVE

GEMINI & AQUARIUS (JAN. 20–FEB. 18)

You love to talk about almost anything, and probably know a little bit about practically everything in the world. Your Aquarian lover, however, may know everything. So, although the two of you can have a wonderful intellectual rapport, your styles are different. You're more flexible. Your Aquarian mate can be rather rigid. Nonetheless, you like being with your partner, and never tire of the repartee. Ultimately, you're compatible with Aquarius and can create strong bonds that make you the very best of friends. You are usually willing to engage in fun and entertaining activities, and your Aquarius partner is a great comrade who is willing and ready to try pretty much anything new and different. You have a persuasive effect on Aquarius and may try to talk him or her into delving into previously unexplored avenues. Together, your agile minds prefer to widen the vision by engaging in such topics as space, sci-fi, or anything unusual and intellectually stimulating. This is an enduring platonic union that can turn into love if the chemistry is right. It will probably take strong connections between Venus and Mars in your compatibility charts for the relationship to develop in the physical and romantic realms.

GEMINI & PISCES (FEB. 19–MARCH 20)

You can tap dance your way through clever conversations as if life was an ongoing cocktail party. Your Pisces lover, however, prefers a quiet world of spiritual thought, exotic imagination, and vivid fantasy. While you push forward into the world with confidence and versatility, your partner gently leans into new experiences with uncertainty and sensitive compassion. You have to speak outwardly whereas Pisces requires time to reflect inwardly. As each of you brings a unique personality into this relationship, you will both need to adapt a flexible approach to life. Flexibility is your middle name, but your partner may be difficult for you to read, so you won't know which way to turn. If you have strong contacts between the Moons in your individual charts, you will be more sensitive to each other's needs. Your Fish can teach you how to weave magic and words into ideas with a new awareness and sensitivity. Meanwhile, you encourage Pisces to rise above the water and peek out at a diverse world, helping him or her discover new vistas of experience and fulfillment. A mutually satisfying relationship develops as you each adapt to the different approach the other carries through life.

ABOUT THE AUTHORS

RICK LEVINE When I first encountered astrology as a psychology undergraduate in the late 1960s, I became fascinated with the varieties of human experience. Even now, I love the one-on-one work of seeing clients and looking at their lives through the cosmic lens. But I also love history and utilize astrology to better understand the longer-term cycles of cultural change. My recent DVD, *Quantum Astrology*, explores some of these transpersonal interests. As a scientist, I'm always looking for patterns in order to improve my ability to predict the outcome of any experiment; as an artist, I'm entranced by the mystery of what we do not and cannot know. As an astrologer, I am privileged to live in an enchanted world that links the rational and magical, physical and spiritual—and yes—even science and art.

JEFF JAWER I'm a Taurus with a Scorpio Moon and Aries rising who lives in the Pacific Northwest with Danick, my double-Pisces musician wife, our two Leo daughters, a black Gemini cat, and a white Pisces dog. I have been a professional astrologer since 1973 when I was a student at the University of Massachusetts (Amherst). I encountered astrology as my first marriage was ending and I was searching for answers. Astrology provided them. More than thirty-five years later, it remains the creative passion of my life as I continue to counsel, write, study, and share ideas with clients and colleagues around the world.

ACKNOWLEDGMENTS

Thanks to Paul O'Brien, our agent, our friend, and the creative genius behind Tarot.com; Gail Goldberg, the editor who always makes us sound better; Marcus Leaver and Michael Fragnito at Sterling Publishing, for their tireless support for the project; Barbara Berger, our supervising editor, who has shepherded this book with Taurean persistence and Aquarian invention; Laura Jorstad, for her refinement of the text; and Sterling project editor Mary Hern, assistant editor Melanie Madden, and designer Gavin Motnyk for their invaluable help. We thank Bob Wietrak and Jules Herbert at Barnes & Noble, and all of the helping hands at Sterling. Thanks for the art and ideas from Jessica Abel and the rest of the Tarot.com team. Thanks as well to 3+Co. for the original design and to Tara Gimmer for the author photo.

Tarot.com

A $5 GIFT CERTIFICATE
FOR YOUR CHOICE OF ASTROLOGY REPORTS OR TAROT READINGS!

Courtesy of Tarot.com for owners of
Your Personal Astrology Guide

Tarot.com is privileged to be the home of master astrologers Rick and Jeff, who are among the few living astrologers capable of writing an astrologically accurate book like this.

Because you have purchased *Your Personal Astrology Guide*, we want to honor you, too, by inviting you to experience your personal astrological makeup in much deeper detail. Visit us for reports written for your unique birth chart by Rick, Jeff, and other world-class astrologers.

To redeem your Gift Certificate, go to
www.tarot.com/freegift2012
Your $5 Gift Certificate is simple to use, totally free, and there are no obligations

 TAROT.COM for Rick and Jeff's FREE horoscopes